SADDAM'S PRIVATE ARMY
HOW RAJAVI CHANGED IRAN'S MOJAHEDIN
FROM ARMED REVOLUTIONARIES
TO AN ARMED CULT

Saddam's Private Army

How Rajavi Changed Iran's Mojahedin from Armed Revolutionaries to an Armed Cult

A. SINGLETON

IRAN-INTERLINK (UK)

Saddam's Private Army
How Rajavi Changed Iran's Mojahedin From Armed
Revolutionaries to an Armed Cult
Copyright © A. Singleton 2003

First published 2003 by
IRAN-INTERLINK

ISBN 0-9545009-0-3

Printed by Antony Rowe Ltd.

CONTENTS

Preface   vii
About The Author   ix
Introduction   xi

Part One From Prison to Ideological Revolution
Historical Context   1
Rajavi's First Bid For Power   13
National Council of Resistance   22
Foreign Relations   31
Armed Struggle   37
Internal Relations   42
Ideological Revolution   54

Part Two From Ideological Revolution to Cult Status
Internal Relations   65
Armed Struggle   84
Foreign Relations   99
Rajavi's Second Bid For Power   110
Internal Relations   121
National Council of Resistance   137

Part Three The Mojahedin in the Present
Dissent Within The Mojahedin   157
Political Scene   171
Glossary   183
Bibliography   185

PREFACE

When this book was written, the Mojahedin were attempting a comeback in Western political circles, and it seemed right to provide interested people with greater information than has previously been available about who they are. Now however, the war in Iraq has negated all the Mojahedin's efforts, and their future looks bleak indeed. At the time of writing, it is not known what will happen to them. Given the intimate relationship between the Mojahedin and Saddam Hussein's regime it is possible to state with some certainty that they will not be able to continue in Iraq with their army as they have before.

There are various scenarios which can be guessed at which will result from the war: The best case scenario for them is that they are re-integrated by the West and accepted back as an opposition to the Islamic Republic of Iran. The worst case scenario is that they are attacked by allied forces, suffer loss of life and are captured as prisoners of war. The reality is likely to be something in between.

Rajavi himself has declared that his army will launch an all out attack on Iran should the allies declare war on Iraq. But with allied troops already cautious about the joint border with Iran this is unlikely to come about. Instead, it could be that small lightly armed units of up to five people attempt to cross the border into Iran. In this case, it is quite possible, considering the recent Iranian reformists' stance on the Mojahedin, that these units would be captured and returned to their families rather than being imprisoned or killed. Another scenario which could unfold would be that the Mojahedin bases are attacked in the north by Kurdish fighters who seek revenge against them. Again, given the control exerted by the allied forces, this is unlikely to develop on any but a piecemeal basis. The most likely scenario, given the Mojahedin's past record, would be surrender to the allied forces and an attempt to do a deal which would allow them to preserve the organisation in Iraq fairly intact, if unarmed. Of course this depends on how much they help Saddam in the war and how much they engage in fighting the allies during the war until Saddam's regime collapses.

Massoud Rajavi has steered the organisation through several damaging crises and has survived. Although it is hard to envisage the Mojahedin remaining the same as now, it is almost certain to survive in some form or other and Rajavi himself, will no doubt be at the head of it still.

Whatever ensues, the current situation points to a radically diminished future for what started out as a heroic and popular struggle for the freedom of Iran from foreign domination, reactionary Islam and monarchy. But the demise of the Mojahedin cannot be blamed entirely on their enemies as I hope this book will show. The organisation itself accepted self-destruction when it allowed Rajavi to pervert the original concepts and analyses which underpinned the ideology. The senior members of the Mojahedin are as complicit in this corruption as Rajavi himself. It is they who bolstered his ambitions and hadn't the courage to say no.

I have written about the Mojahedin from the perspective of someone who had close observation of their inner world. This is certainly not the same experience as those who have lived through it, and I have no doubt that there will be strong reaction to what I have written from those most intimately involved. In my experience it is rare to find anyone who is neutral about the organisation. Indeed, I would regard this as one of the positive outcomes of this book if it helped to dispel the fear which many have of speaking out about their experiences. The more people speak about them the more facts will emerge. History itself will judge them. *(April 2003)*

ABOUT THE AUTHOR

The author was born in Leeds in 1958 and graduated in English Language, Literature and Creative Writing from Sheffield City Polytechnic. Working as a computer programmer she has been an active human rights campaigner for many years with a particular interest in the Middle East and Iran.

Having been introduced to the Mojahedin's activities in 1978 whilst a student, the author took a close interest in the events of the 1979 revolution in Iran. This interest continued with the worsening human rights situation there. The author continued to have close contact with the Mojahedin's activists in the United Kingdom, and attended many of their meetings and demonstrations. Such was the level of trust which developed that she was invited to visit their safe houses in the UK over a number of years, and was peculiarly placed thereby to study from the inside, the organisational changes which took place over two decades.

The close relationship that she maintained with the Mojahedin organisation also allowed the author the unique opportunity to visit their bases in Sweden, France, Germany and the United States of America, where she was able to spend various amounts of time observing their personnel and studying their activities in different sections. This included two trips to Iraq in 1991 and 1992 to observe their military capacity and training.

This book is the result of a unique insight into the secret inner world of the Mojahedin over two decades.

INTRODUCTION

The Mojahedin-e Khalq, or as they are also known in Western circles, the People's Mojahedin Organisation of Iran, remain the largest and most powerful external opposition to the Islamic Republic of Iran. The Mojahedin fields its own army, the Iraq based National Liberation Army of Iran (NLA) and uses as a political alias, the National Council of Resistance of Iran (NCRI). Collectively these are referred to by the Mojahedin as the Iranian Resistance. The personnel of each is comprised largely of the same people. The Mojahedin, NLA and NCRI are led by one, self-appointed man, Massoud Rajavi.

In spite of being labelled as a terrorist entity by the governments of the USA, the UK and Europe, the Mojahedin continues to operate unchecked under its NCRI alias, allowing it to lobby and win the political approbation of the parliaments of those countries. This raises the immediate question as to why this gap exists between the support given by individual politicians and the official government line. Unfortunately there doesn't appear to be a simple answer. While the governments have been accused of political cynicism and the parliamentarians are said to be acting out of ignorance, neither response can be dismissed by such raw arguments. In reality, despite these respective positions, the Mojahedin remain something of an enigma in Western political circles. Neither supporting them as 'the sole democratic alternative' to the mullahs, nor attacking them as terrorists, effectively addresses the issue of who they really are and what they represent.

To add to the problem of how to assess the Mojahedin, the exiled Iranian community takes a completely opposite view from the West's. Whilst any Western political support gained by the Mojahedin is dismissed as simply a propaganda exercise, there has been strong protest against the terrorist labelling, even among those Iranians who most strongly oppose the Mojahedin.

Inside Iran, the political scene is gradually rising to boiling point, with the balance of power between the various factions within the framework of the Islamic Republic of Iran, at stake. This political conflict between the 'reformist' and 'conservative' factions, is represented in turn by President Mohammad Khatami and the Supreme Leader Ayatollah Ali Khamenei. But although these factions are locked in a power struggle to serve and preserve their own interests, clearly what is driving the conflict, are the demands from a society, which has suffered enough repression and deprivation. A society that is now demanding that change (largely in the form of economic progress) comes more rapidly and is more about their needs than the needs of the 'revolution'.

In spite of the dangers apparent in this power struggle, for Iranians who lived through the 1979 revolution, this represents a positive shift in the country's troubled past two decades. Most people felt passionately toward the injustices in their country during the 1960s and 70s, but felt largely powerless to change things. When the revolution did eventually erupt, there was for many, an implicit trust in fate. Perhaps they believed that, as historically a shah had been replaced by the next shah, this time he would be replaced by a democrat. It was an easy delusion to fall into. Now it would appear that these same people are beginning to understand that a democracy is not created by the imposition of democrats on a society, rather it is the process of struggling toward democratic government, which matures people into democrats. It is this process which now appears to be underway again in Iran. After more than two decades, it begins to look like democracy is on the horizon for Iran.

The period in Iran's history since the 1979 revolution can be compared to the historical path toward democracy in other regions of the world during the same period. Yet in many ways, the events remain completely unique. The Shah left Iran not because he didn't know how to rule, or was too dependent on the USA or even because he and his family were corrupt. It was rather for the simple reason that the historical time for Iranians to be ruled by one family had come to an end. The political evolution of the Iranian people had reached a point at which they clearly recognised what they didn't want, even though they appeared unsure as to what they did want. As with any populace, there was no single, cohesive and universally popular solution.

Although the nation had reached a level of political sophistication for which the next step would be democracy, it was never going to be that simple. For one thing, Khomeini was not a democrat. He never claimed to be one and couldn't have made the claim even if he had wanted to. In addition, how was it possible for anyone taking over in Iran, particularly following a revolution that had swept away a monarchy which had ruled the economic, cultural, social and political life of the country for thousands of years, to claim to be a democrat? More importantly, if the definition of political democracy is very loosely defined as accepting a share in power, then anyone who had the platform of 'winner takes all' could not be considered a democrat; no matter whether that person is, in the end, the winner or the loser.

In Iran after the revolution, two people took up this platform. Khomeini who supported the stance 'The only Party is the Party of God', and Massoud Rajavi, leader of the Mojahedin, who later announced his intention to have 'either everything or nothing'. To this day, their loyal followers are supporting these slogans. Through the passage of time, both sides have shown that they will stand by what they have said. Clearly this is why no peace treaties or summits, or even a ceasefire have been agreed, as has been the case in other armed conflicts, such as in Algeria, Sudan, Turkey and Latin America, in which concessions have been made by both sides in the struggle for power.

It is this intractable stand off which has made Iran's path toward democracy, unique and difficult, until now. Even though it is possible to state that in the short run Khomeini has won and Rajavi has lost, it is clear that both sides have irrevocably lost ground and that a third 'democratic' force is emerging and has the support of the people. As such, this force is the real winner. The path of Iran toward democracy could have been very different and followed a more predictable path – in relation to other countries' experiences – had Khomeini and Rajavi seen their future and started thinking about having 'something' rather than losing everything.

In the West, the Mojahedin are a dark horse in Iran's equation of power. On one level their political platform shows them as liberal, pro-Western and capitalist, with a strong emphasis on women's rights. Some of their Western supporters refer to them as 'Iran's democratic opposition'.

In an otherwise informative article *Who are the People's Mujahedin of Iran?* [*] Justus Leicht claims that:

> 'there is little that separates them politically from the so-called "reform wing" of the mullahs.'

But this raises an important question about the Mojahedin. Let us assume that the reformist Khatami received his electoral mandate from a populace looking for a leadership which would return their country to the world community, produce economic growth and development, and impose the rule of law to curb the excesses of those in power, and bring a little democratic accountability. If the Mojahedin's political platform actually offered even half of this, then surely they would have had massive support from the Iranian people, and the election of Khatami would have been unnecessary, as there already existed a force which could deliver the people's will.

Leicht, however, goes on to say that the Mojahedin

> 'stubbornly deny that there are any conflicts whatsoever within the regime.'

This points more accurately to their actual political approach. This describes Rajavi's true platform, which is to have 'everything or nothing'.

---

[*] World Socialist Web Site 14th September 2000 (www.wsws.org).

The Mojahedin ignore the schisms when talking about the regime, because it is in their interests to continue to treat the Islamic Republic as a single indivisible entity. Rajavi can only have everything, if everything that is there now, is swept away in a second popular revolution and his own system replaces it in its entirety.

For two decades, the Mojahedin enjoyed a huge amount of support from Western governments in their armed struggle and propaganda battle against the Iranian regime. The Mojahedin organisation in the guise of the National Council of Resistance, continues to win support as the 'sole democratic alternative' to the regime, from the US Congress, the US House of Representatives, the British Parliament and some of Europe's parliamentarians. But now the governments of all these countries have labelled them as terrorists. Whether this labelling is simply a cynical political manoeuvre to allow closer relations with the Islamic Republic, is consequently a matter of some conjecture.

When it began in 1965, the Mojahedin tapped into a feeling in the Iranian psyche, which said the country, had had enough of dictatorship, monarchy and imperialist domination. With its strongly anti-imperialist stance and the assassination of six American advisors in Iran, the organisation attracted mostly young radical and educated Muslims. By the time the 1979 revolution was underway, many more sectors of Iranian society were willing to support them, including rich merchants. The country began to divide into reactionary and traditionalist Muslims who lined up behind Khomeini, and a whole spectrum of Muslims with informed and progressive beliefs and outlook. Aside from the Liberal movement, which attracted intellectuals, the Mojahedin presented the only channel for such people. So much so, that two years into the revolution, the Mojahedin were able to gather half a million people onto the streets of Tehran at only two hours notice, for the massive demonstration in June 1981. This demonstration became the pinnacle of the Mojahedin's activity in Iran.

After this, Khomeini ordered a bloody crackdown on any and all opposition to his rule. The Mojahedin were forced to go underground and many leading members fled abroad to carry on the struggle from France, which offered them a safe haven.

In the two decades since then, the Mojahedin have both grown in influence and died in support. Today they are shunned and even feared by Iranians at home and abroad. At best they are regarded by the youth of Iran as an anachronism, in much the same way that for the young founders of the Mojahedin, Mohammad Mossadeq, whose star had risen and fallen in the early 1950s, had become an irrelevance in their armed struggle for freedom. At worst, Iranians see the Mojahedin as dictators in the making. 'If they behave like this now, what will they do if they come to power?' is the rueful phrase greeting each new revelation of the Mojahedin's activities.

But their political influence is apparently as strong today, if not stronger than it was in the early 1980s. In non-Iranian circles, and in particular in the West, the Mojahedin are viewed much more sympathetically than by their fellow countrymen. For many people, the issue is clear and straightforward; the Mojahedin profess the desire to bring democracy to Iran and they are struggling against a regime with a horrific human rights record, the Islamic Republic of Iran. The Mojahedin above all, advertise their respect for the rights of women. So much so that they only give specific leadership roles to women in the organisation in order, they claim, to redress the historical imbalance of gender power.

Conversely, the Mojahedin righteously and articulately point their accusing finger at the Iranian regime as misogynist, operating a gender apartheid, and as practicing the worst aspects of what they describe as Islamic fundamentalism. That is, gross violations of human rights, the assassination of political enemies, and the denial of political and social freedoms to the people. This regime, say the Mojahedin, is a total perversion of the true, progressive Islam that the Mojahedin follow.

But to lead the analysis of the Mojahedin organisation down the path of which version of Islam they promulgate would be to ignore the one very dangerous characteristic, which renders it unacceptably dangerous per se. The danger from some organisations or countries is clear: terrorism performed against

Western interests and societies. No one could dispute that this has no relation to democratic principles. Yet the danger posed by the Mojahedin is not so clear. Their Western educated, middle class 'diplomats' visit Western parliaments, academics and human rights activists, with a democratic platform ideally suited to gain the utmost sympathy. The sinister nature of the Mojahedin's real agenda is one not immediately recognised by those examining their political or religious motivations.

One of the main criticisms of former members of the Mojahedin, concerns the internal structure of the organisation. It is described as operating an iron discipline over its members, to the extent of practicing serious violations of human rights in an attempt to make members conform. However, the description of 'iron discipline' fails to adequately convey the behaviour of the Mojahedin towards its members. After all, armies depend upon an iron discipline in order to fight wars. But former members know that the control exerted on them is not the same as that of a classic army. Even though most former members know that they have been in what has been described by many, including the US State Department, as a personality cult, they lack the tools to describe what this means.

In fact, according to Ian Haworth of the Cult Information Centre, all cults share the same characteristics. The definition of any cult is that it indoctrinates its members; forms a closed, totalitarian society; has a self-appointed, Messianic and charismatic leader; believes that the ends justify the means; and its wealth does not benefit its members. He also states that recruits are a certain type of person; intelligent, idealistic, well educated, economically advantaged and intellectually or spiritually curious.

The Mojahedin have all these characteristics, and it is the use of well-documented psychological mind control techniques, which the former members describe as 'iron discipline'. It is a view of their structure, which has not been given much attention until now. The inner world of the Mojahedin, if it is enquired into at all, is still a mystery to Western observers, and it is a deliberate policy of the Mojahedin to keep it that way. Because of this, little importance has been attached to this aspect of their organisation. Yet cult culture is one of the most dangerous forms of society. Firstly, because it robs the members of their most basic of human rights. The Mojahedin has conducted forced marriages and later forced divorces, and has separated children from their parents and had them fostered by their supporters in various countries. But there are even more disturbing issues emerging from the secrecy of their inner world.

In January 2001, a group of fifty Iranians were taken from the notorious Abu Ghraib prison in Baghdad, to the border with Iran where they were secretly exchanged for Iraqi prisoners of war. The Iranians were not prisoners of war, they had been sent to Abu Ghraib prison without legal process by the Mojahedin and the Iraqi Secret Service, after they had expressed criticism of the organisation's policies. The Mojahedin had full knowledge of the deal with Iran. As far as they were concerned, these people were being sent to almost certain death. This was the latest in over a decade of accusations from former members of the Mojahedin who have complained of terrible human rights abuses inflicted on them whilst under the jurisdiction of the organisation.

Amnesty International in its 2002 Annual Report, being unable to investigate in the Mojahedin's headquarters and camps in Iraq, the hundreds of accusations of human rights abuses which had reached its office, resigned itself to stating:

> 'There were unconfirmed reports that the People's Mojahedin Organization of Iran, an armed political group, ill-treated its own members at a base in Iraq. The reports were denied by the organization but it failed to provide substantive information to allay AI's concerns.'

The second, perhaps more imperative reason that cult culture presents such a danger, is because it renders its members obedient to the point, as was seen with the disaster in the World Trade Centre in New York, where they are capable of the most extreme and unthinkable acts of self-sacrifice. Could this be one of the reasons that governments have placed the Mojahedin on their lists of terrorist organisations? Or have they still a more conventionally defined analysis of the Mojahedin based on their missile attacks in Iran which have killed and injured several civilians. Or perhaps the fact that the Mojahedin's armed wing, the National Liberation Army of Iran is funded, trained and supplied by Saddam Hussein in Iraq, is a major consideration. This book seeks to examine these issues and although no definitive answers emerge, it is hoped that this examination will form the basis of a more realistic and in-depth appraisal of the Mojahedin's place in current Iranian politics.

Iran is one of the very few countries in that region which holds democratic elections. Each country holds these elections within a very narrowly defined constitution or system of rule. In Iran, this is based on the preservation of Islamic rule. In Israel, it is the Jewish faith, which defines the state; Israel was founded as, and remains, the Jewish homeland. But their citizens have the power to vote in secret ballots for their choice of leader within that framework. As the years have passed since the 1979 revolution in Iran, the sharing of power has shifted from the autocracy of Khomeini, to a mangled mire of power struggles between hard liners and reformers which involves every single aspect of government and law in the country. What has certainly become clear in all of this, is that once the slightest space opened up for their voice to be heard, the people of the country shouted out. Via the ballot box, they demanded more democratic accountability by their leaders, and for the rule of law to apply to all.

But for the Mojahedin who claim to believe in democracy, none of these count. They don't want to see gradual change emerging from the involved struggles of the people. They want to control the scene and impose their own government on the country. Their army is waiting on the border to do just that. The leader of the Mojahedin, Massoud Rajavi, wants to replace the Islamic Republic with what? With a secular democracy? How does he intend to implement that? More importantly, as the spiritual leader of the Mojahedin, could he resist the temptation to become the new Spiritual Leader of Iran, replacing Khomeini and Khamenei? How can the leader of a cult become an effective leader of a country? These are questions, which need to be examined in evaluating the Mojahedin.

This book does not set out to be a history of the Mojahedin organisation, although it charts the organisational changes chronologically. The book is divided into two parts. Part One leading up to the 'Ideological Revolution' and Part Two describes what happened afterwards. This dividing point is of the highest significance. Regardless of how the Mojahedin present themselves to the outside world through the NLA or the NCRI or the new National Solidarity Front to Overthrow Religious Dictatorship in Iran, the Mojahedin only obeys its internal dynamic, which is the need to keep all the members loyal and obedient.

The mastermind and owner of all the Mojahedin's aliases and activities is one man, Massoud Rajavi. It was Rajavi who engineered a complete rewrite of the organisation's ideology in 1985 with his 'Ideological Revolution'. With that he took control of the organisation and transformed what had been a political organisation led by a twelve member Central Committee, into an ideologically based cult, with himself as the sole leader. Though ironically it is probably the use of cult culture which has preserved the Mojahedin, while most of Iran's other external opposition has diminished or dissolved in the difficult conditions of exile. Rajavi's main asset is undeniably the unquestioning devotion of his followers, which he is able to use in disregard of the normal constraints imposed on political organisations.

This book examines how Massoud Rajavi promoted himself beyond accountability, and how he converted what had been at one point, one of the most popular and powerful armed resistance movements in the world, into a deceptively dangerous cult. A cult which has only its own massive propaganda machine and a few terrorist acts, to preserve it as what is now a very real threat to the process of democracy in Iran. In this respect, the book argues, the Mojahedin in current Iranian politics, fulfil the same function outside Iran as the hardliners do inside. There is a growing movement inside Iran toward democratisation within the existing framework of the Islamic

Republic. It is daily becoming clear that no matter how slight this voice for change is, it represents the real voice of the Iranian people. The only people who wish to stifle this voice are those vying for total power over Iran. Those people are the hardliners, and the Mojahedin who pitched themselves against Khomeini over twenty years ago and who are still fighting to gain 'everything or nothing'. It remains to be seen whether the voice of the people is more powerful than the gun.

Part One
From Prison to Ideological Revolution

Chapter 1

HISTORICAL CONTEXT

The CIA coup, which restored Shah Mohammad Reza Pahlavi's monarchy in Iran in 1953, heralded a dark era in Iranian history. With the defeat of Mossadeq's popular government, the people's perception became that of an Iran dominated by imperialism, exploitation and despotism. An uprising in June 1963, led by Ayatollah Ruhollah Khomeini over the Shah's intended reforms to land and women's rights, was suppressed with guns and tanks. The swift brutality, with which the uprising was dealt, was a warning to all: the Shah would use all means at his disposal to protect his social, economic and political reforms from the plots of communism and reactionary Islam.

Khomeini failed to mobilise the masses at this time over the issues of land reform and rights for women. In this respect, he was out of touch with both the undercurrent of progressive thinking which informed Iran's political scene and the interests which his fellow clergymen had in land ownership. The Shah believed the protests were short-lived, and that once he had exiled Khomeini, his rule would enjoy public endorsement.

However, when Khomeini left Iran, the void was quickly filled by Iran's radical youth, who were inspired by the Marxist ideology. They saw that Marxist organisation and strategy had been effective in helping the liberation movements of other oppressed people around the world at this time. The newly emerging revolutionary guerrilla movements in Latin America and Asia were finding Marxist ideology useful in guiding their struggle. Iran was no different. At a time when the only protest seemed to come in the voice of reactionary Islam, young people responded readily to the appeal of this new form of struggle. Perhaps the revolution in Iran evolved out of the zeitgeist of the age. Maybe the Shah was not overthrown because of what he had personally done, but because the time for change to the whole political system in Iran had come, and the left-wing revolutionary communist inspired groups, were leading the way.

But the appeal of Islam was not dead. Young radical Muslims were convinced that Islam still had a part to play in modern politics and that for too long, the reactionaries had cornered the market in Islamic slogans. In 1965, five university graduates responded to the challenge.

The People's Mojahedin Organisation of Iran founded in 1965

The Mojahedin was founded in 1965 by university students and graduates Mohammad Hanif-Nezhad, Saied Mohsen and Ali-Asghar Badi'Zadegan. Other founder members were Mahmoud Asgarizadeh and Rasoul Meshkinfam. They spent six years studying and developing an ideological framework, mixing Shiite Islam and Marxist theory, to create a radical interpretation of Islam to suit the needs of their struggle. Only then did they start their political activities, that is, revolutionary armed struggle. Once the Mojahedin started their armed struggle, they lost no time in assassinating those who in their view, were the real representatives of imperialism in Iran, American personnel. This original anti-imperialist platform is one, which the organisation has more recently tried to hide, but it still continues to be part of the ideological framework of the organisation.

In his book, *'Revolutionary Islam in Iran'* Suroosh Irfani describes these beginnings:

> 'The Mojahedin did not begin their military operations
> for another six years, even though they had carefully
> screened and recruited over 200 members. These

members were required to undergo an instructional programme in ideology that could take up to two years. During this period, the Mojahedin recruits studied the Qoran, Nahjol Balagha, the book of speeches and statements by Hazrat Ali, and Islamic history. They were also required to acquaint themselves with contemporary revolutionary experience by studying the Algerian, Cuban, Chinese, Russian and Vietnamese revolutions, and develop a critical understanding of Marxism. Next in the instructional programme was military training. Several pioneer Mojahedin were trained in Palestinian camps in Jordan, some of them enriching their experience by fighting alongside the Palestinians against the Royal Jordanian Army in 1971 during the "Black September" conflict.'

One of the first recruits was a young undergraduate in political law at Tehran University, Massoud Rajavi, who joined the organisation in 1966. Rajavi, along with Hanif-Nezhad and Ahmad Rezai, became a member of the ideological group; a study group for developing Islamic parallels for the Marxist ideas which were so popular at the time. He also became part of the sixteen-member strategy team.

In 1969, aged twenty-one, Rajavi was made a member of the twelve member Central Committee of the organisation. His rapid promotion in the organisation was noted by many whom found his behaviour at odds with the ethos of humility and self-sacrifice, which governed the members' involvement. For Rajavi, what was important was his own progress He never cared about other people's circumstances. Hanif-Nezhad remarked at the time that Rajavi had become 'inflated like a balloon' and that he would become more and more big headed with the amount of reading he did. While Hanif-Nezhad had to nag the recruits to read the required books, Rajavi had already read all the books that the others hadn't finished. Hanif-Nezhad said then that it was obvious this would give Rajavi a distorted idea of himself.

Basis for the Mojahedin's struggle

The Mojahedin's success very much depended on their analysis of the failure of past popular movements in Iran, as summed up in their own publication, *Mojahed*. The analysis inspired young people who were extremely critical of the handling of previous struggles and protests. It wasn't even important if people didn't fully understand the implications of the analysis, it was enough that it condemned the past and appeared to present a new methodology for radical change.

According to the Mojahedin there were four main currents of analysis:

1. In the past, people had joined a movement with the aim of removing a 'corrupt' ruler at the top and replacing him by a 'just' ruler. These movements were, therefore, essentially of a reformist nature and those leading the movements lacked a thorough understanding of the nature of their enemy. Occasionally the people succeeded in changing a minister or sending their own representatives to Parliament. But these successes were ephemeral and never succeeded in ending the corruption and poverty prevailing in society.

2. Because religion had played an important motivational role in these movements, they could be termed religious, but they were not ideological. An ideological struggle had to rest upon an adequate theoretical framework; a system of thought which could answer the needs, the problems and questions facing the people. It also had to deal comprehensively and adequately with the philosophical inquiries of those adhering to that ideology. For example, questions like 'What is Man?' 'What is Islamic Economy?' 'Who are the infidels (kafirs) and why killing them is justified?' and 'Who are the hypocrites (monafeqin) and why killing them is justified under the current circumstances?' needed to be dealt with coherently and scientifically.

    Similarly, questions about the origin of the Universe, or the philosophy of history required to be answered by a system of thought that claimed to be an ideology. Hence, given that the previous movements were not ideological in this sense, they were not able to answer the social problems facing contemporary man. And even though these movements were motivated by religion, they reached a dead end because they lacked a long term strategy and organisation. Moreover, since these movements were directed only against an obvious symbol of despotism or injustice – the 'bad man' at the top – they could not have gone beyond the demand for superficial reforms, which would leave the more subtle and deeper contradictions unresolved.

Lacking the organisational framework of a clearly defined ideology, these movements had an inherent weakness, which eroded their capacity for obliterating despotism, exploitation, and imperialism. More importantly, the ideological deficiency of these religious movements was one of the reasons for the indifference with which a substantial section of the intelligentsia viewed Islam and also for their reluctance and failure to take seriously, Islam's revolutionary potential.

3. Previous struggles had failed because they lacked adequate revolutionary organisation and structure. In each instance, the movement had relied entirely on one person only for its leadership. There was no leadership cadre or group that had devoted itself wholly to the struggle as its principal task, taking it, as it were, as a full time enterprise. Nor was there a group that had trained itself concerning problems and issues confronting the leadership. As a result, when the focal figure of a movement, its leader, was eliminated or removed from the scene, it marked the end of that movement, as had been the case with Mirza Kuchak Khan (1906) and Mossadeq (1953).

4. In any case, the leadership of past movements lacked a scientific knowledge about revolutionary resistance and struggle. As a result, it couldn't maintain a continuous, stage by stage, understanding of the social movement or evaluate its effectiveness, and redesign its strategy and tactics. In other words, 'revolutionary struggle' (or 'the movement') had not been approached as a science with its own body of

knowledge and its own methods. As a result, struggles in the past had not enjoyed precise strategy and policy.

In the context of Iran's recent political history, this analysis was astoundingly attractive to young Muslims who had felt let down by their leaders. It is useful to examine this analysis briefly, as it provides a touchstone for charting the changes that Rajavi subsequently forced upon the organisation.

The first item is about achieving power. The Mojahedin's ideology was based on the concept of the total overthrow of the prevailing system, rather than reform from within. In their view, this could only be achieved by violent revolution and this is the justification for armed struggle. This is still Rajavi's aim. His slogan became 'all or nothing'. He cannot share power, but requires that the present ruling system be removed in its entirety, and replaced with his own Islamic democratic republic, led by himself. All of Rajavi's manoeuvrings and strategies have been based on this analysis regardless of the actual changes that have taken place inside Iran over twenty years. And regardless of the will of the people; which has shown itself reluctant to embark on any further revolutionary action in spite of severe repression, preferring instead to challenge the existing system in an attempt to wrest from it some democratic share in power.

Item two refers to the Mojahedin's books that Rajavi has now banned inside the Mojahedin. Books like *'Economy in Simple Words', 'the Path of Man and the Path of the Prophets', 'Evolution'*, etc contain the pure communist message with an Islamic interpretation. The organisation, as can be understood from these books was, therefore, based on sharing and giving everything to the organisation and taking from it as little as possible. This later made the basis for Rajavi's cult. The most basic examples of revolutionary self-sacrifice are the giving of money, possessions and time. These began as revolutionary ideals and were perverted by Rajavi into cult behaviour.

Item three is the most revealing of Rajavi's deviation from the Mojahedin's original ideology. This analysis clearly points to the need to have a group of competent people at leadership level, any of whom could be replaced should they fail in their duty to the people, be killed or otherwise removed. Rajavi has now established himself not only as the sole leader, but also as even more than this; he is a self-appointed ideological leader who is above the law. He cannot be voted in or out, and he now occupies a position beyond democratic or any other accountability. As such, the organisation now exists only in his person, everyone else is dispensable. Yet the original slant of the Mojahedin's analysis was that the people are the permanent feature and the leaders should be replaceable.

Item four describes the necessity for using scientific methods to chart the social movement. Instead, Rajavi has removed his organisation as far away as is possible from the social movement in Iran and has thereby lost touch with the Iranian people. The best use he has made of scientific methodology is in the psychological methods employed to inculcate the members of his organisation into his cult.

1971 – Leading members imprisoned

In 1971 SAVAK engineered mass arrests of the organisation's members, including Rajavi. Over seventy-five members were arrested. Ahmad Rezai was the only top member who remained outside prison at this time and was therefore effectively leader of the Mojahedin. However in 1973 he killed himself with a grenade to avoid arrest, and became the Mojahedin's first martyr in the armed struggle.

The members were tried in a military tribunal and sentenced to death. Rajavi's brother, Kazem Rajavi, a highly respected academic in Switzerland and at one time ambassador to African countries for the Shah, started an international campaign to have the death sentences of all the Mojahedin prisoners, but in particular Massoud Rajavi, commuted to life. He gained support from many prominent human rights activists and academics. However, in spite of his efforts, in 1972 all the Central Committee members except Rajavi, were executed. It remains unclear why Rajavi was the only one spared execution, since international pressure was for leniency to be shown to all the leading members. What made him a special case? Rajavi himself may have unwittingly given the answer to this enigma.

7

In Paris, several years later, Rajavi, as part of his drive to manipulate and indoctrinate his membership, urged Mojahedin ex-political prisoners to ask themselves what they had given for their freedom. His intention was to imply to them that only those who had been executed or tortured to death, had retained their ideological purity; if you survived it meant that you had weakened and somehow co-operated with the Shah's or Khomeini's regime. Clearly, if this really was the case, then this applies just as well to Rajavi as anyone else.

1975 – Splits in the Mojahedin –
Rajavi takes up role of leader in prison

Massoud Rajavi was in the main, regarded by those around him as the most competent member to take up a leadership role for the Mojahedin in prison. However, after the arrest and execution of the Central Committee, many of the members and supporters, who remained outside, went their own way. One group in particular denounced the Islamic ideology and appropriated the Mojahedin name as a purely Marxist group. They murdered some of the leaders and workers of the Mojahedin who were continuing the struggle outside prison and brought the organisation to the brink of collapse. This coup became known as the 'pseudo Left opportunist deviation'.

> '...the Marxist members while justifying the take-over of the central committee of the Mujahideen-e-Khalq organisation reasoned that they could violate the commonly accepted and acknowledged principles and regulations of the organisation because they had evolved to what they perceived to be a "more substantial and evolved ideology" '. (Mojahedin founding document.)

> Extract from *Revolutionary Islam in Iran*, Suroosh Irfani

The Marxist Mojahedin clearly regarded themselves as more progressive than the Islamic Mojahedin and in this way justified their attempted take over. Significantly, they argued that the original Mojahedin ideology had been out-stripped by their newer version.

The Islamic Mojahedin, led by Rajavi, answered this with a quote from the founding document:

> 'If any member of a guerrilla organisation begins to believe that his own individual point of view and conviction is more evolved and developed than the overall ideological foundation of the organisation, and on the basis of this belief feels that he is justified to do as he pleases with other members of the organisation, then, no scientific and rational rules and principles would be left for constituting the common ground for members of an organisation. In that case everyone in the organisation would consider it permissible for himself to commit any crime he pleases.'

Extract from *Revolutionary Islam in Iran*, Suroosh Irfani

It is ironic that Rajavi took such great pains to preserve the original organisation and ideology, only to appropriate and deviate from it for his own use later. The behaviour described above has been acted out in full by Rajavi, who firmly believes that his own point of view is more evolved and developed than the original Mojahedin ideology. However, the original analysis doesn't take into account the possibility that such an individual would exert his control to the extent of making the organisation a cult. This means that everyone in the organisation now apparently considers it permissible for Rajavi to commit any crime he pleases, without necessarily arrogating that right to him or herself. It seems that the pseudo Left opportunists were merely the forerunners of a larger betrayal of the original ideology.

The in-fighting between the Islamic Mojahedin and the Marxist Mojahedin, continued until after the revolution, when the Marxist Mojahedin changed their name to Paykar and operated from Kurdistan where they still exist as a small group.

Rajavi, from inside prison, denounced the change in the ideology and with a handful of other prisoners, stood by the Islamic version. In prison too, however, some disagreed with Rajavi's version of the ideology, such as Lotf'ollah Meisami. Meisami had joined the Mojahedin at the same time as Rajavi and had undergone the same ideological training. He had been arrested when a bomb he was making exploded. In prison he was denied medical treatment for his injuries, which led to blindness and the loss of his right hand. He disagreed with Rajavi over the interpretation of Islam and Rajavi, acting as the leader, expelled him from the organisation. By force of personality, Rajavi led the organisation from inside prison.

At this time, Marxist groups analysed the Mojahedin as 'petit bourgeoisie'. Other Muslim groups saw them as Marxist at root and didn't want to co-operate with them. Khomeini, while in exile in Najaf, Iraq, never clashed directly with them, but nor did he accept to help them either. The only prominent cleric, who supported them both before and after the 1979 revolution, was the progressive Ayatollah Taleghani, who was also imprisoned by the Shah for his beliefs. The Mojahedin tried to utilise his support to the full after the revolution, but he died shortly afterwards, in September 1979.

1979 – Rajavi, freed from prison takes up role as spokesperson

Rajavi remained in prison until the 1979 revolution and was freed on 20th January, being one of the last political prisoners to be released. From the time that he was released from prison, Rajavi took up the most prominent role, that of spokesman for the Mojahedin. He gave his first public speech just four days after his release. This allowed him to gain authority, both within the organisation, and in the public's perception. At this time, there were a handful of other Mojahedin members who were as ideologically competent as Rajavi; Meisami for instance, who was expelled from the organisation inside prison when he refused to give in to Rajavi, and Mousa Khiabani who had also undergone the original ideological training programme.

During the presidential election campaign in 1980, the following were introduced as 'leadership cadre': Massoud Rajavi, Mehdi Abrishamchi, (Rajavi later married his wife) Abbas Darvari (who is now with Rajavi in Iraq, but with no responsibility), and Mousa Khiabani, (one of the original recruits of the Mojahedin and therefore, like Rajavi, had undertaken full ideological instruction. He was killed by the regime after Rajavi went to Paris.). Other leading members included Parviz Yaqoubi who later denounced the Ideological Revolution and was put on trial in Paris and expelled, Mahmoud Ahmadi and Mansour Bazargan.

But Rajavi had advantages over these other leaders. Darvari was a worker by trade and relatively uneducated. Abrishamchi was educated, but in Chemistry; a good qualification for making bombs, but not for political analysis, planning or for public speaking. Khiabani, although an enigmatic figure, possessed true revolutionary humility and fought shy of personal publicity. Rajavi, however, had studied political law at Tehran University. He also came from an educated family; two of his brothers were doctors, one a top academic. This background gave him the confidence and the ability to speak in public. He also had what the others hadn't and which Hanif-Nezhad had recognised; an overreaching sense of his own importance.

Rajavi used this public platform to develop the 'charismatic' speaking style which he would later use to convince his followers that it was his right to act as their sole ideological leader and they had no use for God any more because Rajavi could fulfil that role for them instead!

Events quickly unfolded that allowed Rajavi to take more and more control of the organisation. Indeed, after the revolution, it became necessary to have a charismatic figure at the forefront of the organisation as a counter to the figure of Khomeini. Rajavi and the Mojahedin ideology appealed to radical Muslim youth in a way that Khomeini, in spite of being 'leader of the revolution', couldn't. Khomeini's ideas were not for a new generation, but at the same time, Marxism held no appeal for young people with a Muslim background. In the religiously charged atmosphere, Rajavi used this to the full. He presented a dynamic, passionate figure in his public speeches. He spoke at rallies, at universities, at seminars and in sports arenas. He tapped into the sense of injustice many were feeling as the reactionaries violently grabbed power and control over everything.

Very soon after the revolution, it became clear that there were two Muslim forces vying for power; one was Khomeini with his supporters and the other, the Mojahedin with Rajavi as the voice of the organisation. Once it became apparent that Khomeini wanted total power and that, having power, would not hesitate in commissioning any of the dirty work necessary to stay in power, people began to defect to the Mojahedin. In effect, these two men with their autocratic ambitions were locked in a power struggle from the start that only one of them could win.

Anecdotal evidence of Khomeini's willingness to do this dirty work is given as follows:

> 'When the revolution was underway, the mob attacked all public and government buildings. At the national bank, Bank Melli, they arrested the head of the bank Khosh Kish, and threw him into prison. Khosh Kish protested. He had remained at the bank out of duty to the country not to the Shah. He held it to be his responsibility to hand over the country's financial resources to the head of the new revolutionary regime whoever that might be. Not only did the angry mob not understand this, but Khomeini himself had no appreciation of such an action. After years languishing in prison without trial or accusation, he wrote a letter to Khomeini asking for his release as an innocent person. Khomeini replied pointedly to his aide, "Is he still alive?" and this became Khosh Kish's death sentence.'

Chapter 2

RAJAVI'S FIRST BID FOR POWER

The post-revolution power struggle

In respect of the power that Khomeini had at the beginning of the revolution, it could be argued that Rajavi saved the Mojahedin from certain destruction. Of all the other political challengers who raised their heads before and after the revolution, only the Mojahedin remains intact, albeit totally changed.

Once freed from prison, organisations, which had spent the previous decade and more struggling against the Pahlavi monarchy, began regrouping. Those based on 'revolutionary' principles now saw their chance to influence events according to their own analyses. However, what these organisations lacked was political experience and a real platform for government. They also had little in the way of popular support.

Although Iran had erupted in revolution because people knew what they didn't want, there was certainly no cohesive or coherent concept of what should replace the monarchy. People looked toward Khomeini as the 'leader' of the revolution, mostly because those who followed him were organised and able to take decisive action. A huge network of support was available to Khomeini in the shape of the mosques and mullahs of Iran. This enabled the most religious elements of Iranian society to take command of local affairs. These people looked to Khomeini for leadership, and though he refrained from giving direct orders, preferring instead to declare his intention to remove himself from politics altogether, his speeches and phrases were easily interpreted by his followers as permission to take power by whatever means they found necessary.

In February 1979, soon after he was released from prison, Massoud Rajavi visited Khomeini at his home. The Mojahedin saw themselves, not as rivals to Khomeini, but simply as the natural inheritors of the people's demand for change. They believed without question, that they should be involved in the construction of the country's new governance. Khomeini, with sharp political insight, commented on Rajavi's visit saying: 'the boy calls himself the leader'. He had recognised Rajavi's ambition even at this stage and anticipated that Rajavi would directly challenge him for leadership of the revolution.

But Khomeini had his own agenda. Once established as the country's leader, he initiated a systematic campaign to wipe out all opposition. Perhaps his easiest targets were the communist inspired groups, most prominently represented by the People's Fedayeen organisation. Perhaps they, like many had not fully anticipated or appreciated the ruthlessness of Khomeini and they couldn't afford the price a challenge to his power would cost them. They fully understood, however, with their ideologically based analysis, the danger that Khomeini posed to any social or economic progress in Iran. Almost immediately after the success of the people's revolution, the Fedayeen declared armed resistance to Khomeini from Gonbad in Kurdistan. With the declared strategy of fighting his power from the villages of Iran, which was inspired by the Chinese revolution, this gave Khomeini the ideal excuse for suppressing them. They were denounced as counter-revolutionaries, and at a time when Khomeini still had over ninety per cent of the country's support and Islamic rule still held huge popular appeal, the communists were easy targets for extermination.

Rajavi played a more political game and kept the Mojahedin officially unarmed. He ordered the members and supporters not to fight back if attacked. This gave them huge kudos, not only inside Iran, but also in the world community. In particular as Muslims, they were seen to be the innocent victims of

Khomeini's revolutionary repression, a perception that the organisation strives to maintain to the present day. While Mojahedin supporters actually were the real victims, it is now clear that Rajavi ensured the organisation's survival, simply because he was as shrewd and perhaps even more ruthless than Khomeini; allowing his members to be sacrificed for the greater good, which in the long term meant himself.

Rajavi's insight and careful manoeuvring in the dangerous waters of post-revolution Iran also gave him more and more credit within the organisation. He was deferred to on matters of analysis and strategy. He was fielded as the Mojahedin candidate for both the Assembly of Experts and for the Presidency in 1980. But he was still not regarded as the actual leader of the organisation. The organisation itself did not have that structure. The twelve member Central Committee still met and ran the organisation and it was not until 1985 that Rajavi felt secure enough to declare himself sole leader.

The power struggle between Khomeini and Rajavi eventually brought the regime to the brink of disintegration with the mass demonstration of the Mojahedin's forces on 20th June 1981 and the resulting armed confrontation. The demonstration became known as the 'failed coup d'état of 30th Khordad'. Some analysts define this event as the one which tipped Khomeini's regime over the edge of a post-revolutionary power struggle, into years of absolute repression. Certainly it was the beginning of the end for the Mojahedin inside Iran.

1980 – War begins between Iran and Iraq

In 1980, in the midst of the emerging power struggle between Khomeini and the Mojahedin, Iraq invaded part of the south of Iran and war erupted between the two nations. This placed the Mojahedin in a very sensitive situation. If they continued to oppose the ruling regime, they could be accused of and more importantly be perceived by public opinion of betraying and compromising the nation's security. Consequently, the Mojahedin did try to send forces to fight at the war front to resist the Iraqi invasion, but this conflicted with the army and the massive numbers of Revolutionary Guards and Hizbollah, who were keen to prove their own self-sacrificing credentials in the same arena. This combination of forces couldn't accept yet another force with its own leaders, just as the Mojahedin would not accept the army's command.

The Mojahedin never actively engaged in the war because they wouldn't agree to join with the existing forces and instead declared that they would fight independently if given the opportunity. They pitched some tents behind the front line to cook some food and camp out for a while until it became very clear that they were there for the purpose of propaganda and were not serious about actually fighting in the war. The Mojahedin presence at the war front quickly became untenable and they withdrew.

The Mojahedin's 'political phase' – leading up to 30th Khordad

All this time, month after month, meeting after meeting, the Mojahedin were winning the popularity stakes in the country for their stance against the reactionary led regime's repressive measures. Rajavi's analysis was acute and correct. He understood Khomeini; mostly one suspects because he had the same agenda and the same ambition for sole leadership. He could out-guess Khomeini and being in the role of victim, David to Khomeini's Goliath, he was able to court public opinion just enough to make the Mojahedin a very real threat to the continuation of Khomeini's strangle hold on power. Rajavi ordered Mojahedin supporters to take what he dubbed a 'principled course of action', a phrase he used over and over in the next few years.

It came to signify Rajavi's demand for total obedience in the organisation. In this context it meant that no matter to what lengths the reactionary forces that supported Khomeini went in order to violently intimidate the Mojahedin, no one had the right to return the use of violence. Rather, the young supporters who were on the streets selling newspapers and pamphlets, when faced with gangs of club wielding thugs must submit to being beaten and knifed. They performed this task heroically even though several were killed and tens of hundreds were severely injured and maimed. The Mojahedin referred to this as the 'political phase' since they remained officially unarmed. Yet in all this time, the Mojahedin were arming themselves as rapidly as they could. According to Rajavi's analysis, a showdown was inevitable.

Khomeini insisted that a share in power was possible for the Mojahedin, if they would lay down their arms and close down their militia. A quasi negotiation process continued for some time as the Mojahedin rejected any disarmament. Rajavi didn't trust Khomeini as he knew Khomeini couldn't trust him. The violent attacks on the Mojahedin by Hizbollah (Party of God) simply increased as they were gaining more popular support. Under the intense pressure of these attacks, the Mojahedin declared that they would like to hold a rally and come to see Khomeini along with some of their supporters. It was an attempt to expose him as being responsible for the attacks; to provoke and somehow involve him directly. Khomeini in response, simply said there would be no need for that; 'if they lay down their arms, I will come to see them!'

Support from all sides

The violent attacks inflicted on the Mojahedin came from various reactionary groups which were quite obviously backed by Hizbollah. The government of Mehdi Bazargan and Abol Hassan Bani Sadr, had little real power or influence with Khomeini and his close allies; men such as Ayatollah Beheshti one of the top theorists of the regime.

During the initial power struggle, the whole system was militating against the liberals. In spite of the fact that Khomeini's first designated president, Abol Hassan Bani Sadr was politically a liberal, the word 'liberal' became a kind of swear word associated with imperialism. In this atmosphere, the Mojahedin controversially declared that the real enemy was the reactionaries and not the liberals. Part of their strategy for confronting Khomeini, was to try to bring the liberals onto their side.

17

The Marxist groups' interpretation of the power struggle was informed by their ideology. They interpreted Khomeini politically as 'petit bourgeois', while to their mind, the liberals in Iran were closely allied with imperialism. It was a matter of principle for them to back Khomeini on the issue of the 'liberals' because they analysed Khomeini as being ultimately 'reformable' within the framework of their anti-imperialist struggle. According to their own ideology, the Mojahedin, of course, should have interpreted the scene similarly and shunned the liberals. Massoud Rajavi, however, had no such qualms of principle. He saw himself, not in an ideological but in a personal battle with Khomeini. It didn't matter to him who was on his side if it gained him a degree more power. He clearly believed, even at this early stage, that the ends justify the means. Of course, as will be seen later, he had no intention of sharing any of this power with the liberals or any other person or party that backed the Mojahedin at this time.

In their attempt to garner support from all corners, the Mojahedin started to form a coalition against Khomeini with the liberals and others. The coalition never succeeded as the Mojahedin's demands of this coalition were always too high, and from the other side, Khomeini with power over everything, would not allow such a threat to develop. Of course, this idea of a coalition was useful for some time longer. Outside Iran it became the basis for the National Council of Resistance of Iran. However this also, even beyond Khomeini's reach, did not succeed as a real coalition. In the end, Bani Sadr left the NCRI when Rajavi made approaches to Baghdad. Bazargan didn't even agree to leave the country with them or to support them, though he was openly critical of the way Khomeini dealt with them.

Even years later, when Bazargan came out of Iran for medical treatment and shortly before he died, the Mojahedin sent messages to him asking him to stay outside and work with them. He replied: 'tell Rajavi I have and will have only one wife and I love her very much'. This was interpreted by some as a cutting reference to Rajavi having left his wife in Iran after the failed coup d'état of 30th Khordad and shortly after her death, marrying with Firouzeh Bani Sadr, then in quick succession marrying Maryam Azodanlou, wife of his best friend. Others interpreted his comment as referring to Iran as his wife. But however his answer is interpreted, Bazargan, like many others, refused to join forces with the Mojahedin, even though he criticised Khomeini for the way he handled them.

Ayatollah Montazeri too, the designated successor to Khomeini, was critical of Khomeini's treatment of the Mojahedin, but he never accepted to meet with them. His critical stance led to him being denounced by Khomeini shortly before he died. He was sent to internal exile in Qom, where he remained until his release at the beginning of 2003. Montazeri insisted, like many others, that the Mojahedin represent a way of thinking, an ideology, which cannot be eliminated by killing them and should be dealt with in terms of challenging their thoughts and exposing their ideas. Killing would only increase their numbers. On the basis of this analysis, it could be argued that the present day Mojahedin have become so depleted exactly because of the destruction of their ideology from within rather than the effects of killing and imprisoning them.

30th Khordad – turning point in the power struggle

Once Khomeini had rebutted every attempt to expose him and implicate him in reactionary, undemocratic and repressive measures, the Mojahedin were forced to abandon their 'principled course of action', the 'political phase', and progress to their final, ongoing, strategy inside Iran, that of armed struggle. They began by co-ordinating a more organised challenge to the club wielders. Large, spontaneous demonstrations were held in which tens of hundreds of their supporters spilled onto the streets of Tehran. The regime began to get jittery. Armed Mojahedin personnel were present at some of the demonstrations. It was a challenge to Khomeini's pretended tolerance of their tactics.

In September 1980, the Mojahedin held an openly armed demonstration. This was a surprise for Khomeini, and taken unawares, his forces were unable, or perhaps unwilling, to crush it with the force necessary to ensure there would be no repeat.

The Mojahedin were testing the waters. Rajavi's analysis was that the regime was weak and becoming more fearful of the Mojahedin's challenge. The organisation began to escalate these spontaneous confrontations; pitching large demonstrations at the authorities in an effort to catch them off guard and to force their hand. Khomeini wouldn't rise to the bait so easily. The Mojahedin were playing with fire. After several months of these demonstrations, circumstances forced their hand with disastrous consequences, not just for the Mojahedin, but for the whole country.

By April 1981, the Mojahedin felt confident enough to hold a protest march in Tehran with 150,000 of their supporters, some of them armed. Again, the regime's suppressive forces were not authorised to act and in spite of skirmishes and injuries, the march ended without any major upset.

The Mojahedin, however, were facing a rapidly changing situation. The presidency of Bani Sadr had looked more and more shaky, until in May 1981, Khomeini had found it necessary to dismiss him. The increasing threat that the Mojahedin posed encouraged Khomeini's supporters to even greater acts of violent suppression against the Mojahedin. They were being forced to think of using arms to fight back. But for Rajavi, this would mean the end of a carefully planned strategy for exposing Khomeini's involvement and swinging public opinion massively against him in favour of the Mojahedin.

The intensity of the struggle and the desperation of his supporters compelled Rajavi to make his move. By 20th June, the Mojahedin felt confident enough of public support to stage a defining demonstration. With only two hours notice, half a million people converged onto the streets and marched, chanting slogans, with fists punching the air, towards the parliament building, the Majlis.

The demonstration was clearly a direct challenge to the power of Khomeini. He ordered his forces to open fire. The demonstration was violently dispersed and hundreds were arrested. The next day, after summary tribunals, thirty people were sent to the firing squad, including some under-age girls. Weeks of arbitrary arrest and imprisonment followed.

Executions were performed daily, with no respect for age or circumstance. The weeks turned into months, then into years. The regime, led by Khomeini, went into overdrive in a post-revolution spree of arbitrary killings and torture, and was revealed as one of the most brutal of the past century. For the Mojahedin, and Rajavi in particular, it spelled the failure of their bid for power. A new order had emerged and they were forced to go underground and to change their strategy. Khomeini had won the power struggle.

Chapter 3

NATIONAL COUNCIL OF RESISTANCE

Foundation of the National Council of Resistance of Iran

After the defeat of the 30th Khordad demonstration, the organisation was forced to go underground. But it was too big, and no contingency had been made for the members or supporters in the event of failure. Only the leading members had safe houses to escape to. The vast majority of supporters were left to be arrested or killed. Later their names were to be published in a book as the 'martyrs of freedom' by the Mojahedin.

The regime cracked down on any kind of opposition with mass, arbitrary arrests and extrajudicial executions. This was the end of pretending for all sides. Khomeini showed his true face to the world. Rajavi was about to show his. On the scale of things, little attention was given by the West to the scheming that was to take place in Paris. But the ever increasing alienation of the Mojahedin from Iranian society was about to begin.

The Mojahedin Central Committee had immediately instructed Massoud Rajavi to leave the country in order to take news of their struggle to the world and gain international support and publicity. Mousa Khiabani was left in overall charge inside Iran. Several days later, the international media was covering a story about Massoud Rajavi and ex-President Abol-Hassan Bani Sadr landing at a Paris airport in an Iranian fighter jet, piloted by one of the ex-Shah's personal pilots, who had since defected to the Mojahedin. Accompanying Bani Sadr, Rajavi had made certain that his arrival would not go unnoticed.

Abol Hassan Bani Sadr, the first President of Khomeini's rule, was politically a liberal. He found it increasingly difficult to accept the killing and suppression, which was being conducted through Khomeini's power and influence. Day by day he became more distant from Khomeini. His newspaper took up a similar stance to the Mojahedin, in pinpointing the danger to establishing a representative government as coming from within the Islamic forces, in other words, the reactionaries. Inevitably, in May 1981, because of his reluctance to back revolutionary measures, Khomeini dismissed Bani Sadr as President.

With the defeat of the Mojahedin on 30th Khordad, (20th June 1981), Bani Sadr could see that his time also, and that of many other liberals, had come to an end and that this failed coup would be used against him, either to draw him closer to Khomeini and his policies or that he would be further sidelined and eventually persecuted. The Mojahedin for their part, had ordered their militia to attend Bani Sadr's speeches posing as his supporters in order to encourage him to turn more and more against Khomeini. After 30th Khordad, clearly this 'support' would not be tolerated. Caught between Khomeini and the Mojahedin, the heat created by both sides was too much for any liberal to survive. Bani Sadr decided to take his chance with the Mojahedin organisation, which he trusted, and which in the end, betrayed him.

The Mojahedin had done their utmost to separate Bani Sadr from Khomeini and bring him to their side, even though he did not share the same values as they. This was pursued to the point that a major upset erupted among the Mojahedin's supporters, even in America and Europe where they believed that Bani Sadr should be supported unconditionally by people declaring their allegiance to the Mojahedin, rather than in disguise as Bani Sadr's supporters. This internal criticism was especially strong after the announcement of the National Council of Resistance of Iran and the treaty, which was co-written by Bani Sadr and Rajavi. The Mojahedin were forced to send envoys to the United

States and Europe to talk to their supporters in the Moslem Iranian Student's Society, and were even obliged to expel some of those who could not be convinced.

The same conflict of ideas had also occurred during the Mojahedin's 'political phase'. In this case, posters of Khomeini were displayed in the Mojahedin offices and people were writing articles and letters in his favour. This behaviour was a continuation of the Mojahedin's initial approach to Khomeini's leadership following the revolution, which was to accept it and work with it. It was, of course, a useful tactic for Rajavi in order to delay the confrontation between the Mojahedin and Khomeini. But many supporters believed in what they were doing and even at the start of the 'military phase', posters of Khomeini were still displayed in the meetings outside Iran. These and other issues presented constant internal challenges to Rajavi and the path he wanted to steer the Mojahedin organisation along. At each stage he had to argue and battle with the views of others for control of the scene.

Shortly before leaving Iran, the Mojahedin made an agreement with Bani Sadr to form a political coalition. The first political act therefore, which Rajavi instigated once he was safely in Paris, was the formation of the National Council of Resistance of Iran, the NCRI, which was formally announced on 30th July 1981. This was hugely important in his strategy for the Mojahedin, perhaps more so than he realised at the time. The NCRI, according to Rajavi, was to act as a united front against Khomeini, to advance the Iranian people's democratic movement, and to prevent opportunists from taking advantage of the hiatus of power in Iran. It was heralded as a national, popular, all encompassing front. The Mojahedin's idea was that this political democratic front be formed as an umbrella for the energies and influence of popular parties and personalities, while at the same time, their own organisation would continue with the armed struggle inside Iran in order to provoke a popular counter-revolution against Khomeini. This is what they said.

In reality, the NCRI was created for them to show a democratic face to the West who always insisted on dealing with a coalition. It didn't take long for the West to realise that only obedient people were allowed to join the NCRI, and that those who had the slightest criticism or argument were quickly expelled. Privately, Rajavi would say that the history of people sacrificing their blood and some politicians or other taking the fruit of it, has passed, and this time we want to make sure that the people who have given the blood will rule, meaning himself of course. Rajavi had fled Iran on instruction, but this had ensured his personal survival and allowed him to escape the consequences of his failed coup attempt.

The Mojahedin ensnared Bani Sadr to prevent him from acting alone or from joining with another group of people who would steal the advances made by the Mojahedin in building up resistance against Khomeini. For this reason of course, they tried to recruit many others inside and outside Iran. Some of those courted by the Mojahedin preferred to remain in Iran where they saw the real struggle taking place. They started working quietly to encourage and promote the various democratic movements, which have only very recently begun to make tentative inroads into Iran's internecine political power struggle. Others simply refused to accept the Mojahedin's conditions. Some were killed by Khomeini's forces in the backlash to 30th Khordad and some were reluctantly absorbed into Khomeini's regime. Those outside Iran, who refused to join, were subjected to damaging Mojahedin propaganda to make sure that they would not make any alternative in future.

Iranian commentators and analysts wrote much about the content of the NCRI programme, and it has been much criticised and changed since its inception. But in Rajavi's view, none of this niggling over details, had any real significance. In the interviews he gave on the subject, it is clear that what was important for him was that the Mojahedin hang on to their share of power and exclude any other organisation from the equation of Khomeini versus Rajavi.

Outside Iran, this was done under the banner of an 'anti-liberal' revolution, which devoted one hundred percent of their efforts in Paris to meetings, lobbying and publishing their newspapers so that they kept their public position. Internally this phase was explained in terms of the necessity for preserving their revolutionary identity in the face of Western liberal values, but in reality they used all their resources to attack the Iranian liberals who had left Iran, and who might become rivals.

What was of paramount importance to Rajavi, was that each of the NCRI members agree that the Mojahedin representative should take control of the interim government after Khomeini's overthrow. That representative was of course Rajavi himself. This is the fundamental issue that he wanted the NCRI to accept. He remarked 'We were certain that once the correct strategy has been adopted, all the other shortcomings, weaknesses and mistakes would be ratified in due course.' The 'correct strategy', in other words, was that as long as you accept that I will be the interim leader, then all other differences mean nothing and can be resolved in time.

The reaction of other groups was scathing. They attacked Bani Sadr and the Mojahedin. From Monarchists to Marxists to Liberals, none could accept such a proposal and all denounced it. Of course this was what Rajavi wanted; to exclude every body else in anticipation of the victory which he believed was imminent. He believed that he didn't need anybody else (he little suspected that later, even with the help of Saddam Hussein, he would not be able to topple the regime with his military militia (National Liberation Army of Iran) without a proper coalition) and the more they denounced the sectarianism of the Mojahedin, the happier he was to draw his lines. Privately, Rajavi told the Mojahedin that the more they attack us, the easier things will be after our victory because these attacks will be proof for the Iranian people in the future that this is what all these other people did while we were fighting with the regime, and therefore they cannot lay claim to anything.

Publicly, Rajavi dismissed their carping as sour grapes because they had failed to progress their own organisations. This was partly true. It was ostensibly unfair of them to pick on the Mojahedin when in fact it was Khomeini's regime, which had all but destroyed them. Yet there remained a teasing grain of truth in their arguments. There was, consciously or unconsciously, an awareness that Rajavi was up to something more than his words implied. He was regarded as devious and treacherous, but no one could seem to put their finger on what he was doing. Even when they did, their voice was quickly quashed by the Mojahedin's anti-liberalism propaganda machine.

The break-up of the original NCRI

At first, the formation of the NCRI was welcomed by a variety of well-known parties, and personalities. Bani Sadr, as Iran's first post-revolution President, and the Kurdish Democratic Party of Iran, were considered the two main pillars of the NCRI which gave it credibility. The presence of other well-known personalities such as Dr Nasser Pakdaman, Bahman Niroomand, Mehdi Khanbaba, Dr Mansour Farhang and several others, was a major factor in the preliminary success of the NCRI.

However, it wasn't long before Rajavi's demands began to take their toll. The first casualty was the democratic relations between the parties involved. It soon became obvious that Rajavi wanted the NCRI to act as a tool in his hands to serve the aims and purposes of the Mojahedin. Soon only those who were willing to offer loyalty to Rajavi and were willing to follow Mojahedin policies, were accepted into the NCRI.

Bani Sadr became increasingly critical of Rajavi's developing relations with the Iraqi government, which were being facilitated by the Kurdish Democratic Party (KDP). On 24th March 1983, he officially announced his separation from the NCRI. Bani Sadr refused to accept the support of foreign forces in toppling Khomeini's regime, in particular when that force was at war with Iran. Bani Sadr was a man of principle. Just as he rejected Khomeini's use of violence, he now rejected Rajavi's opportunism. In Paris, Bani Sadr was totally at the mercy of the Mojahedin. He was living in Rajavi's house and therefore had no means to do anything without their help. Everything he wanted to achieve had to be arranged through the Mojahedin. It was impossible for him to mount an internal resistance to Rajavi's control of the NCRI's policies.

After Bani Sadr left, it was the turn of the KDP. Rajavi had the organisation ousted from the NCRI on 14th April 1985. The pretext was that the KDP had had contact with the Khomeini regime. In the view of the Mojahedin, this was unacceptable. There was no ground for contact in any shape or form. For the Mojahedin the choice was either us or Khomeini, with no compromise.

But for the KDP, although they viewed the Khomeini regime as an implacable enemy, they still were realistic enough to see that they needed contact. While they were involved in armed conflict, there was need for communication; where and how to return the bodies of those killed, arrangements for exchange of prisoners, etc. These were the realistic communications between two sides at war. The KDP's struggle was not ideological as was the Mojahedin's, but was rather for Kurdish autonomy, yet they preserved their independence, while the Mojahedin did not. They also fully understood the deep responsibility they had toward their people in Kurdistan. The Mojahedin had simply left their supporters to the mercy of the Khomeini regime.

The Mojahedin also contributed greatly to the break up of other organisations, including the communist Fedayeen-e Khalq. These organisations, by giving their support to the Mojahedin, forced many of their members to defect. Such as Mehdi Sameh, who broke up the minority section of the Fedayeen-e Khalq in order to join the NCRI. He joined the Fedayeen to the NCRI in name only, with less than a handful of members. (Their first split into minority and majority factions was really the act of Khomeini. His tactics forced the majority faction to get nearer to the Soviet backed Tudeh Party after the military defeats in their strategy of working from the villages. The minority faction resisted this development, preferring to maintain a purely Iranian communist identity).

Conclusion

The NCRI as it had been originally constructed in 1981, lasted no more than two or three years. After this, there were only eleven members, the largest and by far the most powerful of which was the Mojahedin. Others were either individuals or small organisations whose influence carried little weight.

Rajavi's manipulation of the NCRI for the benefit of the Mojahedin could possibly, if the Mojahedin had been a democratically run political party, have been excused, even praised as being politically astute and pragmatic. But the Mojahedin was based on ideology in spite of the political manoeuvring of its leader. It was not itself a democratic organisation in which the ideas and beliefs of its grass roots members were taken into account. This meant that the coalition was never likely to succeed while the Mojahedin were its most powerful member in terms of personnel and material resources. The Council allowed Rajavi to put a liberal face to his virulently and violently anti-imperialist organisation. It was a means also to absorb and destroy other opposition forces so that the Mojahedin remained the only major force in opposition politics. But Iranians were never convinced of its validity as a democratic coalition. The popular perception was expressed in the phrase 'if they act like this in opposition, how will they behave in power!'

For his part, Rajavi was not only shaping the NCRI for his own and the Mojahedin's benefit; he was, at the same time, consolidating his control over the Mojahedin organisation. The result was seen in the announcement in 1985 of the Ideological Revolution in which Rajavi appointed himself and his new wife, as co-leaders of the organisation. By this time, the NCRI had been reduced to only a handful of members, whether organisations or individuals. Rajavi managed to convince these members of the paramount importance of the continuation of the Mojahedin's armed struggle, and that the NCRI speak with a unified voice when confronting the Khomeini regime. Those who objected were ousted or forced out.

Rajavi found various ways of dealing with the remaining members by manipulating their weaknesses and needs. Those who were most democratic and liberal in their beliefs, though their arguments were probably the most cogent and critical, were actually probably the easiest for Rajavi to deal with. He was adept at arguing the same theme in various ways, which was that as long as the Khomeini regime continued its torture and executions, then no one had the right to speak out against those who were fighting directly with the regime and sacrificing their lives, that is, the Mojahedin inside Iran. This became an impossible position to refute and so the other members of the NCRI were obliged to be circumspect in their criticism of the Mojahedin's flouting of democratic principles and other people's views.

So far, the members of the Mojahedin themselves, were wholly loyal and devoted to their cause. This allowed Rajavi the power base with which to impose his own wishes on the Council. But when he announced the Ideological Revolution in 1985, he faced not only incomprehension from the NCRI members, but a significant amount of confusion and rejection within the Mojahedin itself. His answer was to strengthen his methods of control and manipulation in both organisations. This worked with some, but others left the NCRI leaving it even more depleted and lacking in credibility as a coalition. This situation continued after the Ideological Revolution until Rajavi found a new way to push his aims: transform a large section of the Mojahedin into the NCRI and call it the political wing of the Iranian Resistance. How this backfired on him will be seen in Part Two.

Chapter 4

FOREIGN RELATIONS

When the Mojahedin members were released from prison in 1979, they were plunged into a very different scene to that in which they had taken up their struggle. They emerged in the midst of a popular uprising and quickly set about establishing their influence and credentials. Part of this effort was also directed at the outside world. The Mojahedin were aware that they needed to influence world opinion about their cause. This was something they had learned through the campaign, which Kazem Rajavi had organised from Switzerland in 1972 to prevent the execution of the Mojahedin's leaders and his brother. But at the same time, the Mojahedin lacked any political experience. Because of this, they had the naivety to believe that whatever notice the world took of them, was as a result of their own efforts and not, as was the case, because the world had vital strategic and economic interests to protect in that region and needed to know who might be a help or a hindrance in this protection.

Massoud Rajavi's brothers lived in Europe. His brother Saleh Rajavi, was a doctor in Paris. Using his influence, the Mojahedin began sending leading member Abbas Darvari on frequent trips to Paris to make political contacts and explain their position in order to gain support for their struggle against Khomeini. These contacts eventually stood them in good stead when the Mojahedin lost the power struggle after the 30th

Khordad demonstration. Relations were sufficient at that point, to allow Rajavi to take refuge there in June 1981. Although Darvari and Saleh Rajavi had made the initial contact to secure French support, Rajavi actually went to Paris at their request. Because they had been in prison for years and had no political experience of any kind, when the Mojahedin were given the green light by France to go there, they thought this was something they had achieved themselves.

The West in general was interested in the Mojahedin because they had armed power and a significant degree of popular support, and this was clearly regarded as the optimal way to confront the might that Khomeini's regime wielded. It was thought that after the Khomeini regime had been toppled, Bani Sadr would become more moderate and could be used to keep Rajavi in check. This strategy soon failed because Rajavi followed his own agenda and his alignment with Saddam Hussein, in effect, forced Bani Sadr to leave the new political coalition, the National Council of Resistance of Iran.

In Iran, Khomeini's regime was quickly gaining the kind of notoriety granted to only a handful of dictators throughout history. The killings, which started in earnest after 30th Khordad saw no sign of abating, even after two or three years had passed. The repression was bloody and absolute. The Mojahedin played an important role in exposing the atrocities, publishing photographs of public hangings and accounts of torture, extrajudicial killings and widespread executions. They brought to the world's attention the execution of pregnant women, of children, descriptions of horrific tortures, draining blood from prisoners before execution for use at the war front, and the forced deployment of boys as young as twelve in the war. The savage behaviour of the regime's suppressive agents, made despairing reading. Was it possible for human beings to behave like this in the last quarter of the 20th Century? Fresh boundaries were being set for horror.

In this atmosphere, the Mojahedin found it easy to get support for their cause. Again, in their naivety, they assumed that they had done this. In reality, anyone who was anyone in politics used the Mojahedin to prove their anti-Khomeini credentials. Rajavi's black and white thinking made this easy. Mojahedin members, who indefatigably lobbied every political channel they could find, offered a simple position; if you backed the Mojahedin you were automatically against Khomeini, but you were not against Islam. No other group had such a strongly defined position. No other group ran such a good publicity machine. Governments, opposition parties, unions and NGOs backed them, and not only in words, funding was granted to the Mojahedin on practically any pretext; anything to show opposition to Khomeini.

France itself gave the Mojahedin a base in Auvers sur Oise, a suburb of Paris, with twenty-four hour armed police guard. The expenses at the base were met by the French government, including over 200 dedicated telephone lines to make contact with the organisation's forces inside Iran. Other governments were as generous, West Germany discreetly allowing the purchase and export of a radio transmitter.

For the press and media however, it was a different matter. From the beginning of his residence in Paris, Rajavi, although he courted publicity for the Mojahedin and their cause (that of overthrowing the regime), personally shunned meetings and interviews with journalists. He was afraid of their questions. The difference between his public persona in Iran as spokesperson of the Mojahedin and his retiring persona in Paris was remarkable. As time elapsed and the regime became more and more entrenched in its bloodthirsty work, it appeared that the Mojahedin were making no headway in altering the situation, having, apart from the assassinations of some significant leading members of the regime, only lists of martyrs to show. The press began to probe more deeply into Rajavi's strategies and intentions.

When political people did question what the Mojahedin actually stood for, they were mostly interested in their anti-imperialist stance and how this would impact on Iran if they toppled the regime. Little was known about the internal structure of the organisation. Little attention, therefore, was being paid to Rajavi's internal power struggle. The Mojahedin were still optimistically regarded as an armed, revolutionary and committee-led organisation, which was part of a broad coalition, the NCRI. In this respect, the West saw nothing to fear from them.

Later on, after the failure of the Forouq-e Javidan operation in 1988 and when the Mojahedin had since crushed any other viable opposition force, the West began to withdraw its support. This was exacerbated in 1991, when Rajavi chose to stay in Iraq with Saddam Hussein during the Gulf War. It was a clear choice of ally, which made it impossible for the West to continue their overt support. However, the West retained its interest in the Mojahedin as a bargaining chip to be used against Iran. Much in the same way that Saddam Hussein has always used them.

During the past fifteen years of their stay in Iraq, Saddam Hussein has supported them when he has not been under pressure and then, in a reversal of approach, stopped them using the border to attack Iran in order to gain Iranian support for lifting international pressure on Iraq. Meanwhile they have been very useful for him in intelligence gathering against Iran as well as undertaking some activities in Europe and the USA which Iraq could not do under her own name. The Mojahedin have always provided intelligence to the West about Iran, which was mostly reworked information from the Iranian media. However, because of their close relationship with Saddam Hussein, the Mojahedin have never divulged one iota of intelligence to the West concerning Iraq.

Exiled from Iran, Rajavi was offered a great deal of help from the international community. France gave him refuge and funding. For years the Mojahedin were funded by Western governments and through countries like Saudi Arabia, which used the Muslim Iranian Student's Society in the USA or charities like Iran Aid in Europe, to send their transactions from disguised bank accounts.

In the beginning, the Mojahedin claimed anti-imperialist credentials. However, in the end it was Khomeini who remained faithful to a purely anti-imperialist stance, while Rajavi opportunistically allied himself to all and sundry for his ambitions. The NCRI was a good idea at the time and some important people were involved, such as Bani Sadr, Ghasemlou and Hedayat Matine Daftary along with a few others who separated early on. It could have been a way forward, but for Rajavi, the others were never radical enough, and for the others, Rajavi was too independent and willing to follow his own agenda. Bani Sadr left over the issue of going to Iraq. He refused to go to the country which was attacking Iran and be seen to be siding with Iran's enemy. In many respects this was a correct position, most importantly because of public opinion inside Iran which did not tolerate the action and still refuses to accept it. And also, it placed the main focus of the resistance movement irrevocably outside Iran's borders rather than where it should have been, which is inside the country.

Relations with the Iranian opposition

The phase which led up to the Ideological Revolution in 1985 was called the 'anti-liberalism revolution'. This meant that the organisation worked hard to retain its revolutionary identity. This was to the extent of not even modernising its stationery, except for that of Rajavi of course. The message was 'total opposition to the Khomeini regime'. Any compromise was denounced as a betrayal of the people's struggle. This paved the way for the Mojahedin to destroy any liberal opposition to the regime. Ninety percent of the Mojahedin's time and effort was now spent in finishing off well-known personalities outside Iran. The way this worked was that they either accepted Rajavi's conditions and joined the NCRI, or they were targeted politically by propaganda, by slander and libel. Some were physically targeted and had their meetings disrupted with violent attacks by Mojahedin supporters. This treatment of other Iranian opposition groups and personalities continues to this day, and is the only reason they are able to make the claim as the sole alternative to the regime.

The list of those groups and personalities subjected to Mojahedin propaganda excludes nobody, except the few who had accepted his leadership (and only while they accepted it). Over seventy personalities have been labelled as working for the Iranian Intelligence Ministry because of their outspoken criticism of the Mojahedin, as over 350 of their ex-members have likewise been labelled. Although for a time this had some effect on Iranians outside Iran, as the Mojahedin have become an anachronism in the politics of Iran, these attacks no longer carry any weight. Their carping cannot be taken seriously now. Indeed, their claim accounts for an average of one recruitment by the Intelligence Ministry of Iran every twenty days over the last twenty years!

Chapter 5

ARMED STRUGGLE

Rajavi takes the resources of the organisation to Paris

Immediately after the failure of the 30th Khordad demonstration, the Mojahedin Central Committee agreed that Massoud Rajavi should be sent out of Iran along with Abol Hassan Bani Sadr. They were to take refuge in France where Abbas Darvari had already established contact. Rajavi was sent abroad in good faith by the Mojahedin's Central Committee as the organisation's spokesman. His instructions were to gain support from the international community and to publicise their struggle and ideology. It soon became clear, however, that his own personal survival was as important to Rajavi as anything the organisation required, and the opportunity this escape would give him to hold on to the power he had already gained.

When he left Iran, Rajavi took with him as many as possible of the organisation's resources; the administrative, printing, financial, and personnel resources. Supporters inside Iran were instructed to send gold, jewellery, carpets and any other valuables they could collect, out of the country to fund the struggle. Rajavi himself took with him as many members as possible who could be of value to him in his mission to publicise the struggle and his leadership of it, members who would be loyal to him or could be easily swayed to his way of thinking. He continued to bleed such members out of Iran for some years to come, leaving the internal forces severely depleted and demoralised. But for Rajavi this was not important. Internal forces were useful to him as numbers and blood; as a list of names for his rapidly growing 'book of martyrs'. In Paris, he established what for him, must have seemed a government in exile, and set about publicising his role.

In no other country had an opposition force actually left the country in order to continue its struggle. The Mojahedin sent Rajavi abroad with a specific task – to court international political opinion in their favour. He could have achieved this with very few of the organisation's own resources. France offered him a base and funding. His brothers, in particular Kazem who had campaigned for commutation of his death sentence back in 1972, were in Europe and held positions of respect and influence. In addition, there was already a well organised, professional and very active group of Mojahedin supporters outside Iran, the Muslim Iranian Student's Society. Many Iranian students had chosen not to return home after the revolution, so providing a huge resource of new recruits outside Iran. Rajavi didn't need to take the organisation's own resources. But for many people even at that time, it was obvious he had an inflated view of his position and importance. It could be assumed that he saw himself as the leader at this stage rather than as one of the leading Central Committee members and clearly believed that his court should attend him.

Rajavi bled the organisation in Iran dry in order to set up a government in exile. He had the NCRI agree that he would be the interim leader after Khomeini was toppled, and he regarded this leadership as imminent. This was a big strategic mistake. Rajavi probably did save the Mojahedin in the short term, keeping it alive in a political sense. But he had vastly underestimated Khomeini and in turn overestimated his own and his organisation's abilities.

Armed struggle inside Iran – the 'military phase'

Outside Iran, with all the resources of the organisation with him in Paris, Rajavi declared the strategy of the resistance for overthrowing Khomeini as:

1. Dealing fundamental blows to the regime's ruling figures by assassinating key persons.
2. Going for all out attacks on the machinery of suppression in order to smash the atmosphere of terror and fear.
3. Unleashing the popular element; that is, arranging protests, demonstrations and workers' strikes etc.

All this, in his view, would prove the impotence of the ruling regime.

But how was the Mojahedin to perform all this when most of the leaders and resources of the organisation were outside the country.

In spite of the massive popularity of the Mojahedin, which had grown after the revolution, the number of members who could be described as cadre was still very limited. Only the top members had safe houses to escape to after 30th Khordad. Ordinary members and supporters were left to fend for themselves as best they could. While friends and families and other sympathisers were willing to help and shelter most of these forces, many others were betrayed to the authorities by pro-Khomeini neighbours or acquaintances. In this context, the Mojahedin began using whatever means they had inside Iran to attack the regime's forces.

Having infiltrated the Jomhouri Eslami Party, they put a bomb in their Headquarters in Tehran, killing almost one hundred people, including Ayatollah Beheshti, one of the founders of the Islamic Republic and the closest person to Khomeini. They also planted a bomb which killed the new Prime Minister, Rajai. They then went on to commit suicide bombings, including the killing of Ayatollah Dast Gheib, another prominent clergyman who was again close to Khomeini and an important theorist. These assassinations sent a ray of hope for many whom were looking for a way of defeating the ruling regime. But this did not last long. In February 1982 the regime, through its own counter-infiltration of the Mojahedin, discovered the whereabouts of Mousa Khiabani, the Mojahedin's commander inside Iran, and several other top members including Rajavi's wife. These top members were killed in a gun battle and Mojahedin infiltration of the regime's apparatus was quickly blocked.

After Mousa Khiabani was killed, the Mojahedin appointed Ali Zarkesh, another deeply experienced and committed member, as commander inside Iran. The Mojahedin's forces were able to continue their struggle because they operated as cells which had no knowledge of one another's existence and which were all independently in contact with Paris. Although they were infiltrated, it was not easy to discover other cells and the struggle continued.

At the same time as the forces inside Iran were fighting a guerrilla war with the regime, outside Iran, Iranian refugees were being recruited to fight against the regime. Soon after his escape from Iran, Rajavi had established contact with Iraq's leader, Saddam Hussein using the KDP's existing links with him through their leader Ghasemlou. The KDP and Iraq allowed the Mojahedin to set up training camps inside Kurdistan. Mojahedin members and supporters, who had fled Iran, gathered at these bases in Kurdistan. The new recruits from the West were also sent there, and would eventually form the basis of the NLA.

As the resources were becoming more and more depleted, and the Mojahedin members inside Iran more dispersed, Rajavi's initially damaging strategy deteriorated and weakened. It eventually became more and more limited to shooting pro-Khomeini shopkeepers, placing bombs in garbage bins and shooting targeted individuals in the street in order to keep up the momentum of resistance.

After some time, Rajavi changed his mind and announced a new strategy called 7/7 (seven-sevenths). This meant that the Mojahedin inside Iran should start killing the so-called fingertips of the regime (that is, its suppressive forces such as the Pasdaran or Revolutionary Guards) to such a degree that the regime would be paralysed. It was also hoped that there would be an uprising because people would no longer be afraid to come out and support the resistance. The Mojahedin never achieved even one killing a week, but they did not abandon this theory until the establishment of the National Liberation Army in 1987 and with it the strategy of using an army to topple the regime.

An important feature of the Mojahedin's ability to conduct their armed struggle from outside the country was the use of radio. In 1982 the Mojahedin purchased a 10 kw radio transmitter from Siemens in West Germany. Although it required a class A export licence, they were allowed incognito, to ship the radio and other equipment to Baghdad, and from there, were able to transport it to Iraqi Kurdistan and from there to Iranian Kurdistan. There they enlisted the help of Kurdish villagers to help transport the equipment, by mule and eventually by foot, into the mountainous region where they eventually established their radio base. At this stage KDP membership in the NCRI was useful since the Kurdish villagers helped willingly due to their support for the KDP. It wasn't too long however, only about two years, before the Iranian forces pursuing their war with Iraq forced the Mojahedin to retreat into Iraqi Kurdistan. They took the radio with them and were soon helped by the Iraqi regime which allowed the use of Iraqi radio stations in addition to their own.

The radio was vital for the Mojahedin to broadcast their messages into Iran. It allowed them to recruit new members and to direct their activities. Eventually, they broadcast news of Rajavi's Ideological Revolution. For the young people inside Iran facing imminent discovery and death, this was a massive blow to their belief in the Mojahedin, as they had understood it to be. It seemed not only irrelevant to their struggle, but as a betrayal on several levels. The radio had quickly become a vital propaganda weapon against the regime. But at the same time the effects of the broadcasts on supporters and sympathisers were unmonitored and didn't always have a desirable outcome.

Chapter 6

INTERNAL RELATIONS

The ground for changes to the organisational structure

The Mojahedin's internal structure and organisation at the time of the revolution in 1979 would have allowed the possibility of it eventually evolving into a democratic rather than remaining a revolutionary organisation. After 1985 that possibility no longer existed. From its inception the Mojahedin was governed by a Central Committee, a group of people who were deemed ideologically qualified to lead, and who could be replaced over time by others more competent. The execution of the Mojahedin's original leaders in 1972 left the organisation vulnerable to perversion. At the time of the pseudo-leftist deviation, it was Rajavi who maintained the organisation's Islamic identity.

Inside prison, a core group of members, led by Rajavi, built up trust between themselves, so that upon their release in 1979, they were able to re-establish the organisation's structure and ideology. Rajavi further used this trust to establish the loyalty of these members, and took as many of them as possible to Paris with him, leaving those who might challenge him, inside Iran. Those who accepted this corruption of power inside the organisation stayed with Rajavi and became corrupted in turn. Those who challenged the corruption either left the organisation or were killed in Iran in the ensuing repression.

But in spite of his ambition, there was a balance between Rajavi himself wanting to become leader, and the organisation actually pushing him into this role by its total dependence upon and trust in him. The Mojahedin held him up as the ideological teacher, the representative and Presidential candidate; they praised and fawned around him.

It is arguable, that both culturally and politically, after the fall of the Shah, nobody was looking for the establishment of a democracy. The dominant culture was that of finding a hero to look up to and follow. Now a 'bad' Shah had gone, everyone was individually looking for their version of a 'good' Shah to solve all the problems. There was no culture of collective responsibility and this provided a breeding ground, fair game, for people with ambitions like Khomeini or Rajavi. The same reasoning holds for why the majority of people in Iran followed Khomeini and why many continued to follow him for so long.

Rajavi begins self-publicity

After he was safely out of Iran in 1981, Rajavi was quick to promote himself as the Mojahedin's leader. The subtle tracks of his self-aggrandisement can be found in the organisation's own publications. One early pamphlet is entitled *'Interview with Mojahed Brother Mas'ud Rajavi (one of the leaders of the Mojahedin) about the National Council of Resistance N.C.R. Paris August 1981'*. Clearly Rajavi was still regarded by the organisation as 'one of the leaders'. Soon, in a publication in September 1981 *'Iran – Gains in four months of Resistance – Guidelines for future stages, Message of Brother Mojahed Mas'ud Rajavi to the heroic people of Iran'*, it becomes clear that Rajavi has a different view of himself and his role. In this publication, only four months after the 20th June 1981 demonstration, he describes Mousa Khiabani as

'my deputy and lieutenant in every political, military and organisational aspect.'

Rajavi goes on to urge:

'Pay full attention to his political instructions and his military commands as before.'

This begs the question, before what? It very much appears that by demoting Khiabani to deputy and by default promoting himself to leader, Rajavi feels the need to reconfirm that Khiabani is still in charge inside Iran. But only just. By making the statement he undermines Khiabani's position. In any case it didn't matter much because it was inevitable that Khiabani would be killed sooner or later, thus leaving Rajavi more room for manoeuvre.

The Central Committee members and other high ranking members of the Mojahedin, had no reason early on to suspect Rajavi of plotting to promote himself as sole leader and so were not aware of the import of such statements in respect to themselves. As one of the longest surviving members, they regarded Khiabani, as almost equal to Rajavi in ideological competence. Reference to him, as his deputy had no other meaning than this. It would not have been interpreted at this time as expressing a hierarchy of power as much as the hierarchy of ideological competence, which they all abided by.

A different publication two and a half months after the 30th Khordad (20th June 1981) demonstration, is entitled *'PMOI The message of the People's Mojahedin Organisation of Iran on the occasion of the beginning of the seventeenth year since the foundation of the organisation and the great, historical days of September'*. The 6th September 1981 marked the seventeenth anniversary of the PMOI. The message was published from inside Iran after the foundation of the NCRI. It refers throughout to 'we' as the PMOI and refers to Rajavi in such terms as 'our Brother Mas'ud Rajavi's relentless efforts abroad'.

It is rather sad to see how much trust they put in him and how they viewed him as their saviour. Nowhere does it imply that he is their leader or that they have the notion of such a concept. The document is presented by the PMOI, that is, as an organisation rather than by any individual. This had always been the way until Rajavi started to promote himself as 'The' representative. The space between the abortive 30th Khordad coup until the establishment of the NCRI, effectively marked the beginning of the end of the Mojahedin as its founders had conceived it. After this, everything that Rajavi does is for his own benefit and aggrandisement.

Rajavi's first initiatives in taking control

Once firmly ensconced in Paris, Rajavi started off placing himself further and further away from critical eyes. He would not join with others without thorough preparation first. He delegated work in such a way that there would always be other people to take any ensuing criticism. He only opened himself up for public access when it was time to garner the fruits of the Mojahedin's efforts, such as in interviews, publications in his name, and in meetings in order to show his face in important forums. Rajavi's worst nightmare continues to be that a reporter or anybody, who could challenge him in public, corners him. He has never allowed that to happen. Every interview has to be arranged, recorded and checked personally by him. This has led to many conflicts with the media, which have not accepted his conditions. Rajavi has taken journalists to court or even boycotted the BBC when he could. Whenever there has been a mistake and critical journalists have reached him, the person responsible has been punished. The punishment is usually degradation and humiliation for a period of time, and then sending them to wash tanks or clean vegetables as their new duty. In severe cases, they can be sent to a room for weeks, to write self-criticising reports in order to find out what is wrong with themselves ideologically.

On 8th February 1982, Mousa Khiabani, in charge of operations inside Iran, was killed. Rajavi's wife, Ashraf, was also killed. One of their personal bodyguards had been an informer to the regime, and they were ambushed in their safe house in the north of Tehran. The death of the second most ideologically competent member of the leadership cadre began to open the way for Rajavi. If anything had happened to Rajavi, it would have been perfectly feasible for Khiabani to take over his role as spokesperson. Khiabani was a passionate and moving orator in his own right. It was his additional courage and skill in the military field, which led to him being left in Iran while Rajavi was ordered abroad. As long as Rajavi believed that he could become the sole leader of the Mojahedin – and it is by no means clear at what stage he began to see this as a real possibility – Khiabani represented his biggest threat. His death relieved Rajavi from having to challenge his beloved friend and deeply admired fellow combatant.

When Khiabani and the others were killed in their safe house, Rajavi and Ashraf's son, Mostafa was taken away from the scene and given to Rajavi's parents to care for. Later he was sent to Paris to be reunited with his father with the approval of Khomeini. This is something Rajavi would not have contemplated doing if he had seized Khomeini's son. Mostafa, together with Maryam Rajavi's daughter Ashraf, from her marriage to Mehdi Abrishamchi, grew up in the best part of Paris and received the best possible education. At the same time, other parents in the Mojahedin were required to send their children to the hostels in Germany and elsewhere to take part in the street fund-raising activities for Iran Aid etc.

Rajavi has tried on every occasion possible, to represent Mostafa as his successor, using outrageous arguments such that the succession of the Shiite Imams was from father to son, among others. Mostafa now lives in Iraq and heads a new military regiment for young people – meaning the children of the Mojahedin who have been returned to Iraq – which was established by Rajavi. He is thereby grooming Mostafa for the future to take over from him.

The Mojahedin outside Iran – the organisation he inherited

During the time of the Shah, there was no official representation of the Mojahedin outside Iran. Their literature, including their court defences, were published by the Islamic Student Society which was Islamic based, or by the Confederation of Iranian Students Outside Iran, a secular, predominantly Marxist organisation. A publication named *Mojahed*, was published by Ghotbzadeh (later an official of the regime and killed for alleged involvement in an American plot against the regime) and was distributed by postal subscription only. The publication did not have direct contact with the Mojahedin, but would publish their views as far as possible.

Reza Raisi was one of the close friends of Mohammad Hanif-Nezhad. He had been in close contact with the Mojahedin since its inception and had escaped from Iran when they were being attacked in the early 1970s. He took up residence in London, studying a PhD. in politics. Then, about two years before the 1979 revolution, Raisi started an organisation named Committee in Support of the Mojahedin.

Raisi had highly developed organisational skills and a good background in politics as well as religious knowledge. He was easily and quickly able to establish his new organisation's headquarters in London, with branches in the USA and France. He began recruiting and teaching potentially acceptable members and held classes and discussions as well as activities in order to promote the ideology and political views of the Mojahedin.

At the start of the revolution, they changed the name to the Moslem Iranian Student's Society, later changed to Confederation of Moslem Iranian Student's Societies in Europe and America. These were of course the boom days and suddenly there were branches in every major city and a lot of work was being done, including producing publications in several different languages and reprinting and distribution of Mojahed newspaper in the Iranian communities in the West.

Shortly before 30th Khordad, Raisi visited Iran and met with the Mojahedin there. Up to this point, the contacts had been made by telephone and telex. Shortly into his trip, Raisi telephoned from Iran to his headquarters in London to say that he had some problems and that he would be back in England later than expected. The next day, the Mojahedin called London to say that Raisi had been demoted and no longer represented the Mojahedin. They said they would immediately send someone else.

By the time Raisi returned to the base in London, there had already been visits from two people from the Mojahedin. They had held lectures in which the official message was that anybody who accepts the Mojahedin without question can stay, or else people should go. Since people at the lectures regarded themselves as devoted supporters of the Mojahedin inside Iran, only a handful that felt uncomfortable with this demand for obedience left. In this atmosphere, when Raisi came to the base, nobody was willing to listen to him. He left the base and went back to his studies. Later, Raisi announced his opposition to the way the organisation was being run. Much later he returned to Iran and took up a teaching post at a university, having no further involvement with the Mojahedin headed by Rajavi.

Raisi had created an organisation which was well structured and effective. It encouraged its members to be educated in the ideology and to think and to question and to be actively involved in the progress and development of the organisation. His generous and idealistic nature allowed him to give responsibility to others and to encourage growth and independence in the members. He believed that the members should be encouraged to develop competence both ideologically and organisationally. That is, he believed in a meritocracy in which those who were able were promoted. This contrasts totally with Rajavi's idea that only those who worship him can be promoted.

The organisation was very active and effective, carrying out various programmes aimed at the large Iranian student communities in Europe and the USA. This existing experience and structure allowed the Mojahedin to gain a lot of support after the revolution. They had the facilities, methods and members at their disposal to perform a propaganda coup, which no other Iranian organisation outside Iran was able to match. All the publicity which the Mojahedin were able to gain against the human rights abuses of the regime, were as a direct result of Raisi's organisation's strength.

After Raisi left, the Society underwent a radical reorganisation. The classes and teaching stopped and more activities were programmed. The anti-Khomeini demonstrations in London and other Western capitals were made more and more radical until shortly after that, the order came to seize embassies throughout Europe and the USA. The message was passed down that the Society had been passive and had been too inward looking because of Raisi. Now was the time for action not classes. Members were instructed to either make money for the Mojahedin or get involved in some action such as selling papers, working in Kebab shops, or seizing embassies or hunger strikes etc. As a result, the existing members of Raisi's organisation with local knowledge of their country of residence, were the ones who grew the Mojahedin in the West. It was they who took the initiative in developing these new activities, not the Mojahedin who had come from Iran.

The Mojahedin began selling their newspaper *'News on Iran'* in the street to gain money and to raise public awareness. This progressed to activities such as asking people to give sponsorship money for an Iranian marathon runner. In this way, they were able to raise funds for their activities as the Muslim Iranian Student's Society. This public fund-raising was later transformed into charities and foundations like Iran Aid with a declared annual income of several million pounds, the funds from which were said to be for victims of the regime, particularly children, inside Iran. But in reality, in all their time as fund-raisers, the Mojahedin's charities and foundations throughout the West, have barely used money for anyone inside Iran and have, apart from Iraq and Western governments, been the major source of funding for their armed struggle based from Iraq. The UK's Charity Commission eventually closed Iran Aid charity in 1997 following an investigation into the misuse of its funds in this way.

After Rajavi came to Paris, the organisation he inherited was truly progressive and ideological. It took some time for the Mojahedin to transform this Society into an obedient organisation with little to ask and little to learn. Rajavi's requirement was for a force that would work all hours of the day and do without sleep, and would unquestioningly undertake any kind of task and activity. Thinking or enquiring or learning, became something only for the top members and not something an ordinary supporter was supposed to expect. In the meantime, the policy of cutting roots and ties came to the fore, based on the experience inside Iran. As a slogan it was constantly stressed that the more you give, the more revolutionary you are. This philosophy has been used up to this day; first give all your money, financial investments and possessions including your houses and businesses. Then move into the base and give one hundred per cent of your time. Then give up your spouse and your children and then it comes to your mind and thoughts. You must give everything to the revolution, which means, of course, to Rajavi. Certainly, by the time Rajavi announced his ideological leadership in 1985, the Mojahedin membership outside Iran had become largely obedient and unquestioning.

The recruitment of members outside Iran

After coming out of Iran following the failed coup attempt of 30th Khordad, the loss of supporters in Iran was inevitable. Many were arrested, many killed and many simply became disappointed and went home to get on with their lives as best they could under the new regime. After Rajavi escaped and the rest of the head of the organisation went into hiding, it was only a matter of time before the majority of the body dissolved. But they didn't even try to solve this problem or address it. Maybe this was Rajavi's biggest mistake because it meant losing the trust of the people and it also severed the links to ordinary people.

However, outside of Iran, Rajavi was attracted by a new source of recruitment; ready, inexperienced, willing, and easy to manipulate and fool, were thousands of young Iranian students in the West, who had been encouraged by the Shah's reforms, to study abroad. Mainly from the wealthy middle class, they were left after the 1979 revolution with their dreams shattered, and with no path to follow. Many of them had access to large sums of money which, under instruction from the Mojahedin, they extracted from their parents with lies and blackmail.

For years afterwards, the Mojahedin would encourage supporters and members to lie to their families – saying they needed money for medical or legal reasons – to get as much money as they could from the unwitting families of members. That is after already giving all they had, which in some cases, was a great deal of gold or investments and properties which parents had put in their names.

After the revolution, students who were abroad either went home or found themselves exiled because they were in disagreement with the nature of Khomeini's Islamic regime. This could have been because they were from the class who benefited from the Shah's regime, or because they were against

Islamic rule, or because they were afraid, or for a whole host of other reasons. The expatriates quickly divided up into various factions, which reflected the refraction of society inside Iran. The established organisations, such as the Mojahedin and the Fedayeen, started recruiting. This was not difficult as most Iranians felt passionately about the revolution and more or less aligned themselves according to their interests. Those who were not politically minded and/or were supporters of the previous regime put their heads down and got on quietly with their lives. Some, who supported Khomeini and had ambitions to rise in that regime, returned to Iran or associated themselves with the embassies or consulates. Some students were the children of very prominent mullahs in the new regime. These kept very, very quiet. Things could go either way for them!

Another phenomenon was that the behaviour of these Iranians changed. The disco going, girlfriend-flaunting behaviour was muted and everyone tried to act a little more circumspectly. For one thing, no one was certain when their next funding cheque would arrive as all Iranian banks and assets had been frozen.

So, the Mojahedin, along with the others, started a recruitment drive. The Mojahedin had a huge advantage because of the organisation, which Reza Raisi had started two years before the revolution. It meant that there was already a group of highly organised and committed young people who could be used to garner support. The Muslim Iranian Student's Society was already becoming sophisticated in its recruitment methods and used a sort of emotional, moral blackmail against anyone who showed any interest in their activities. That is, people were drawn in because of the nationalistic argument or because they were labelled as cowards if they didn't do something to help their country and their people. The war with Iraq also helped fuel the nationalistic argument, even though the Mojahedin had no involvement in the fighting.

A great deal of recruitment was achieved through meetings and demonstrations. At every opportunity and at every excuse, they made themselves visible. In universities and colleges all over the West they established Moslem Iranian Student's

Societies. They used the facilities and grants of the Students' Unions to stage their meetings. They attracted people because of the message they gave out and because of the organisational behaviour. It is legendary that many people joined them because the individuals who made up the membership impressed them. The Mojahedin had a 'revolutionary' discipline and principled behaviour, which no other group had, not even the foreign groups, which were also prevalent at that time, such as those from El Salvador or Chile etc. The capacity for devoted self-sacrifice was attractive as a role model for young idealists. Even so, it is important to understand that new members were actively recruited using a methodology rather than simply joining because of their interest.

Once an individual expressed even a little interest or sympathy for the Mojahedin's aims, pressure was exerted in various ways to get them more involved. The most obvious pressure was purely nationalistic. The person should be fighting for the freedom of their country from the despotic grip of Khomeini. It didn't matter whether this person was Muslim or had any leanings toward the ideology of the Mojahedin, what mattered was that the Mojahedin presented itself as the only alternative for them to channel their protest.

In one case the local head of the MISS had someone shamefacedly confess to him after a meeting, that he had been implicated in giving information to the SAVAK whilst an undergraduate student in Iran. This could only have been at the most incidental and inconsequential level because this person had no information to give and couldn't remember to whom he gave names or about whom. Still, the Mojahedin set themselves up as a higher moral order and instructed him to make his confession public in the Iranian community. They wrote a short paragraph on his behalf, that he was a SAVAK agent and was truly penitent and begged everyone's forgiveness. He was required to sign this and then paste it all over his university city so that all Iranians would be aware of this. The Mojahedin then intervened to prevent him being beaten up by angry students. They used this as pressure on this individual to join them, even though he was communist by belief and wanted to remain passive. They claimed that only they could protect him and forgive him. This was another of the Mojahedin's frequent name calling episodes. As far as the Mojahedin were concerned, Iranians were either passive or active in the face of the Khomeini regime. If anyone remained passive, they were derided in such a public and humiliating manner, that many caved in and came along to meetings just to get the Mojahedin off their backs. Some hope. Once embroiled in their clutches it was very hard to get out.

Ironically, at this time it was actually extremely difficult to become a member of the Mojahedin. People had to undergo ideological and organisational training and pass tests in order to be accepted. So, although Iranians were corralled and cajoled into going to meetings and demonstrations and giving time and money to MISS activities, actual membership was held out as a barely attainable greater goal. If you became a member you had really made it.

In fact, it was easy to be thrown out of the organisation for any slight misdemeanour. One student, who was being groomed as a potential member, when working as part of a fund-raising team, was asked in one of the daily review meetings to say what he most enjoyed about the work. His reply, 'watching women' was his – probably much wished for –passport straight out of the organisation. He was never seen again!

After the Ideological Revolution in 1985, things turned around. It began to be much easier to join than to leave. The negative aspect of this can be seen now that right, left and centre the police are discovering infiltration in the Mojahedin's bases. This was happening in Europe in the early 1990s and more recently we read in their newspapers about infiltration in their army in Iraq. Many of their operations have been intercepted because of infiltration in their teams. Rajavi wanted numbers and still does. Who they are and where they came from, does not matter any more. As in the past, he still has to show an increase in numbers, although in reality, he has lost members year after year. Apart from anything else Rajavi is paid by the number of people he declares to Saddam and this is why there are always more guns than people in the camps.

Chapter 7

IDEOLOGICAL REVOLUTION

The Ideological Revolution within the Mojahedin, remains the major definitive event in the organisation's internal history after the 1979 revolution. After this point, the organisation slipped rapidly into cult culture and lost every vestige of normal revolutionary and political identity. So, in simple terms, what was the Ideological Revolution?

In February 1985, a marriage ceremony was performed by Massoud Rajavi and a Mojahedin member called Maryam Abrishamchi (nee Azodanlou) before a gathering of Mojahedin members in Paris. They described their marriage as 'ideological' and explained it thus: Maryam had chosen to divorce her husband and marry with the ideological leader of the Mojahedin, in order to allow them to work in close proximity as co-leaders. Massoud announced that Maryam had achieved a level of competence which demanded that she become co-leader of the Mojahedin, while at the same time, he would retain his primary role as ideological leader of the organisation.

Until this time, the membership had no idea that there was to be a change in their organisational structure let alone the ideology. And even as the marriage was performed, few had any understanding at all of the changes, which being introduced.

The marriage was declared necessary, due to the growth in Maryam's competence and to allow her to hold the position of co-leader. However, the real changes, which were to take place after this marriage, revealed themselves as more to do with Rajavi's ambition to wield absolute control over the organisation and its members. The real aim of the Ideological Revolution was to publicly and irrevocably establish Massoud Rajavi's ideological leadership of the organisation. Which in effect interprets as power. Neither he, nor Maryam were chosen by the membership of the organisation and were both self-appointed. Rajavi, modelling his leadership on the uniquely unassailable leadership of Khomeini, wanted to move himself into a position from which he could not be ousted or challenged, and ideological leader (the equivalent of Khomeini's role as Supreme Leader, or Imam) fitted this bill.

By 1985, Rajavi was secure enough in his position in the Mojahedin for him to undertake this publicly. Mousa Khiabani, who could have challenged his sole leadership on ideological grounds, was dead. Rajavi had manoeuvred and manipulated all the other high ranking members within his reach, to the point where those who accepted this corruption of Mojahedin ideology were loyal to him, and those who objected were sidelined, ousted or allowed to be killed inside Iran.

In 1981, Rajavi had founded the NCRI with twelve members, with the condition that he be appointed as interim leader after the Khomeini regime was toppled. On 8th February 1982, Mousa Khiabani and Rajavi's wife, Ashraf Rabii, were among those top Mojahedin members killed in a gun battle with the regime's suppressive forces in Iran. This left the way open for Rajavi to consolidate his leadership role in Paris. Now he only had people like Mehdi Abrishamchi to deal with and he could do this more easily because they were in exile with him in Paris. After years of imprisonment alongside them, he knew their characters and how to manipulate them, or he knew they wouldn't raise a challenge against him, and if they did, how he could appease them.

Only months after Ashraf was killed, Rajavi had married Abol Hassan Bani Sadr's daughter, Firouzeh. She was a student at a university in Paris at the time. She had no political inclination as far as is known and was largely regarded as being used as a pawn by Rajavi in the manipulation of her father. Ironically, this marriage did not cause any controversy. Members saw it for what it was; a political tactic. Ordinary Iranians saw it as both a convenient and a normal marriage. Rajavi's wife was dead, so why shouldn't he marry again, albeit indecently quickly? Yet this marriage really was cynical and exploitative. The young Firouzeh was naïve and innocent and had no real choice in the matter. Not a very good basis for marriage to a man who later promoted himself as the defender of women's rights in the Mojahedin. In fact it was the next marriage, between two highly ambitious and fully aware people, that caused the outrage and continues to do so. Why? Because Rajavi married his best friend's' wife. (The relationship started long before Abrishamchi was ordered to divorce.) Looking at the marriage from a traditional point of view from Iranian culture, it was dishonourable, a betrayal of his friend. It was wrong, if not scandalous.

In 1982, Maryam arrived in Paris as part of Rajavi's efforts to have as many people as possible leave Iran and join his court in Paris. Although Maryam was not a leading member – at this time women had not become the issue of the moment and were still taking a secondary role in spite of their equal activities – she was important enough to have been fielded as a Tehran candidate for the 1980 elections in Iran. So, particularly as Abrishamchi's wife, she would have been a familiar figure in the leading circle of the Mojahedin.

Maryam was highly ambitious and looking for a way to rise in the organisation at any cost. Rajavi didn't know Maryam very well in Iran. There were many top women members who ranked higher than she in the Mojahedin, most of whom left the organisation during the Ideological Revolution or had remained in Iran and been killed like Ashraf. Maryam was brought out with her husband and daughter when Rajavi tried to evacuate as many people as possible. In Paris, because of her hard work and devotion, Rajavi chose her as the helping hand in his office and to arrange domestic issues and to take care of Firouzeh. She was their housekeeper and Rajavi's personal assistant.

It was not difficult for Maryam to replace Firouzeh for Rajavi. She gave him total obedience and also had a malleable, ambitious mind. She was devoted to the struggle. Firouzeh, on the other hand, had a mind of her own and exercised it freely by doing whatever she wanted. This of course, was unacceptable for Rajavi – who now demands one hundred per cent obedience even from people he isn't married to!

Rajavi said at the time, 'This girl has already got an ideological leader, and that is her father'. Instead, Rajavi needed someone to declare: 'He is my leader, body and mind' and Maryam fitted this role. She would have done anything to gain promotion in the organisation. Her point of view was 'Either he will marry me or I will kill myself.' In this respect it is widely believed that she began a sexual relationship with Rajavi even before he divorced from Firouzeh in 1984. Maryam was practically living-in with Rajavi in his buildings as his personal assistant, hardly visiting her husband at all.

In 1984, less than two years after their marriage, Rajavi divorced from Firouzeh. He married Maryam probably before the divorce was legally finalised. Ostensibly, this divorce was viewed as resulting from the discord and disagreement between Rajavi and Bani-Sadr, but the role Maryam played has not been shown until now. She had been appointed head of Rajavi's office and she worked closely with him in his office, often not returning home at night for days. Before their marriage on 8th February 1995, Maryam hadn't returned home to her husband Abrishamchi for several months. In this time, she had also attended a hospital in Paris for what is believed to have been a termination of pregnancy.

Although Rajavi's divorce from Firouzeh was publicly explained by his disagreement with Bani Sadr, Maryam's ambition led her to create division between Rajavi and Firouzeh, long before this political break-up. She was in a unique position to interfere. It was Maryam's intention to oust Firouzeh, but one that Rajavi found very useful for his own goals. Maryam had two faces, one in the presence of Firouzeh and one for Rajavi. It could be assumed that Maryam had fallen in love with Rajavi with an ideological passion. This is not surprising or unusual.

But what was unusual and highly significant for the future of the Mojahedin organisation, was Rajavi's use of this affair. He could possibly have done a quiet deal and got Abrishamchi to divorce his wife and he could have divorced Firouzeh and the lovers could then have been married and continued in their respective roles. But this did not happen.

It is possible that some aspects of Rajavi's relationship with Maryam had come out into the open and they couldn't carry on quietly as before. But more significant, was that this was the make or break point for Rajavi after all his years of preparation. He was forced to lay his leadership on the line. Either the supporters and members would accept this – and really they would accept anything – and as he said himself 'the taboo will break', or they would reject it and leave. Rajavi has always said that he is only interested in those people who accept him as their ideological leader. For these people, when they accept an ideological leader, sins mean nothing. What he does must be right and good, rather than as they might interpret it; they aren't capable of knowing what is right or good, only the ideological leader can say this.

The Ideological Revolution changed the whole nature of the organisation and what it was about. Probably at this point, the future of the organisation was sealed as being hopeless. Partly because the marriage was seen publicly as something scandalous. Partly because the members of the organisation saw it as a divergence from the original structure and because most people didn't see the relevance in the fight with Khomeini. After all, that was what the Mojahedin was supposed to be doing. This was a defining point in the organisation's history. Nobody could have seen that what was the most significant result of the event was the effect it had on internal relations, which allowed Rajavi to impose a cult culture on his membership.

Immediately after the marriage, Rajavi persuaded Abrishamchi to publish a statement professing that he 'understood the grandeur of this 'epic' with all the ideological might God had given him'. Rajavi then had the other members of the Central Committee of the organisation, under various threats including the threat of withdrawing their financial support, issue a sixteen page edict, explaining the revolutionary necessity of the marriage, eulogising Rajavi's transcendent capacity for sacrifice, and drawing parallels between Rajavi and the prophet of Islam.

It was established during this Ideological Revolution, that if Rajavi wanted any woman, it was his right and the woman's duty. The traditional Muslim story was cited in which the prophet Mohammad looked at a woman. Her husband, believing that the prophet Mohammad liked her, promptly divorced her and offered her to the prophet. With this as the guideline, it became the duty of any of Rajavi's followers to happily get out of the way and sacrifice themselves for his benefit. Abrishamchi was offered a marriage to Mousa Khiabani's younger sister Azar. Abrishamchi was forty years old and she was barely eighteen. They were married straight after the Ideological Revolution.

Rajavi used various arguments to convince the Mojahedin's membership and supporters, of the necessity for the Ideological Revolution. The most prevalent was that 'to fight with Khomeini you have to detest him and to detest him you have to love his opposite which is Rajavi'. This was a great sacrifice for Rajavi to allow himself to be exposed and labelled in order to break the taboo and free everybody and give them the tools needed to fight Khomeini. He had to be prepared for opposition and for members to leave over this issue.

Convincing the membership, as always, followed the same routine of lengthy talking sessions for some and then employing these people in sessions to convince others. Then lastly, to bring in NCRI members to listen to the specially prepared sessions, first saying that this is an internal matter of the organisation and then talking to them one by one according to their individual characters, i.e. using blackmail or bribes as required. Remember these NCRI members had already been convinced about other things. One Iranian analyst even claimed that some of them had accepted Islam even though they were communist because the name of the new government the NCRI proposed to bring to Iran after the overthrow of the Khomeini regime was the Democratic *Islamic* Republic of Iran.

These few individuals had different interests. Some hoped for power, some were simply too involved and compromised to say anything and some were hoping that once this deed had been done, time would pass since the important thing was that they were fighting Khomeini. Some were thinking that in time, they could correct the Mojahedin and make them more liberal. The Mojahedin's principal accusation against people has always been that if you are not with us, then you are with Khomeini. Liberals were under fire and many of these people were afraid of that accusation.

Other people's reactions to the marriage

Public reaction was that this was shameful and simply based on lust. At best, it was irrelevant to the political struggle that was taking place. What meaning did a marriage have in armed struggle? In fact, the marriage had its worst impact in the prisons inside Iran where thousands of Mojahedin members and supporters had been incarcerated and tortured since 30th Khordad. Following news of the marriage, hundreds of prisoners just broke down and gave in because of that. At first they thought it was a fabrication of the regime, just like when they had heard the news of Rajavi's departure to Paris. But when Maryam was declared 'joint leader', they wondered what had happened to the other leaders, the Central Committee.

The move was introduced as a significant step forward in the organisation's ideology, but was criticised by ordinary people as being dishonourable. It was criticised by political analysts as being irrelevant and criticised by members as being deviant from the PMOI's aims. So what was the word from the other leaders?

When he announced the Ideological Revolution, those members still in Iran objected to it and didn't accept it. They were still running the organisation as it had been originally conceived. The most prominent of these objectors was Ali Zarkesh, who was the commander of the organisation inside Iran after Khiabani was killed. After Rajavi realised that Zarkesh could not be convinced and that this could pose a real threat to his plans, he tricked Zarkesh and brought him to Paris under false pretences, where he was immediately demoted. Zarkesh was never accepted back into the organisation in any meaningful way and was kept isolated. Later on, during the Forouq operation, it is alleged that Rajavi had Ali Zarkesh killed.

One of the Mojahedin who was captured during Forouq and imprisoned in Iran, was Ebrahim Zakeri's personal bodyguard. Zakeri was head of Rajavi's Intelligence Services. The captured bodyguard confessed on Iranian TV that he had personal orders from Zakeri to kill Zarkesh during the operation.

Another benefit that Rajavi enjoyed by demoting Zarkesh, was that he could then appoint Maryam his deputy instead of him and push his own agenda forward. Maryam replaced Zarkesh in title, that is commander of the armed struggle inside Iran. But of course, she never went to Iran and so in effect, the Iran section was left without anybody inside the country. Later Rajavi announced the idea that individual teams should be contacted by telephone and therefore there would be no need for a leader inside Iran.

Parviz Yaqoubi, a member of the former Central Committee, was in Paris and married to Ashraf Rajavi's (nee Rabii) sister. He refused to accept the marriage and Ideological Revolution and refused also to keep quiet about his objections. He was put on trial in a court, which Rajavi concocted and headed, and was condemned. He was 'convicted' for not taking the side of the revolution, but rather taking the side of Khomeini. Rajavi in this court on one occasion, refused to accept that Yaqoubi has the normal rights of a court and said this is not a court rather it is a learning session for others to listen and take note. Of course, only selected people were present. Yaqoubi was placed under severe hardship. He was isolated, his financial support from the organisation was cut and he was evicted from his home as an example to others.

Hassan Mehrabi, the tactical mind behind much of the Mojahedin's ideological and political literature, also turned against Rajavi in Baghdad and refused to accept the second phase of the Ideological Revolution, the Internal Revolution in 1990. He was abandoned under great personal hardship and pressure in Iraq. Years later, he was able to return to Paris and get on with an ordinary life, finding work there. He kept quiet and has never spoken about what he knew.

As for the ordinary members, there was a mixture of bewilderment and enthusiasm. For most, Massoud Rajavi could do no wrong, and so the announcement of the marriage and the Ideological Revolution was accepted per se and looked upon as a positive measure. For some, however, this was regarded as a betrayal of the organisation's original ideals. One member was so indignant at the marriage that he set fire to himself in protest at the marriage ceremony and had to be rushed to hospital where he subsequently died. Others displayed their protest by leaving the Mojahedin. Whatever their reaction, it soon became clear that the Mojahedin had undergone a radical transformation and would never be the same again. Just how this would affect the organisation was yet to be seen.

Part Two
From Ideological Revolution to Cult Status

Chapter 8

INTERNAL RELATIONS

The marriage of Rajavi and Maryam created a new order within the Mojahedin. Before this, there were no women at leadership level and the leadership took the form of a committee of ideologically qualified cadre. Suddenly, Rajavi was the leader of the organisation, not the Central Committee. His new wife was elevated above them to the level of co-leader. This had an enormous impact on the membership. Many were dissatisfied and left, or continued to work under protest. How far was Rajavi's move to Iraq and the building up of military forces outside Iran an attempt to absorb this anger into activity? Certainly the culture of the Mojahedin even at that time was such that thinking and reflection was frowned upon and members were kept busy and exhausted to prevent them from focusing their minds on what the leadership was doing. Instead they were required to fight even harder against the Khomeini regime.

The membership and supporters of the Mojahedin were made dizzy by the marriage and Ideological Revolution and they had not been pre-warned of such a move. In fact, Rajavi's tactic is always the same, and that is to divert attention by external actions when he wants to do something extraordinary inside the organisation, or when he is facing a big defeat, such as operation Forouq-e Javidan presented in 1988.

This chapter is best understood in the context of the quote from the Mojahedin's founding document which Rajavi previously used to answer the breakaway Marxist element in 1975:

> 'If any member of a guerrilla organisation begins to believe that his own individual point of view and conviction is more evolved and developed than the overall ideological foundation of the organisation, and on the basis of this belief feels that he is justified to do as he pleases with other members of the organisation, then, no scientific and rational rules and principles would be left for constituting the common ground for members of an organisation. In that case everyone in the organisation would consider it permissible for himself to commit any crime he pleases.'

Extract from *Revolutionary Islam in Iran*, Suroosh Irfani

The new order within the Mojahedin

The message of the Ideological Revolution was simple. Maryam had been promoted above the heads of all the other leading members because of her unquestioning devotion to Rajavi. She gave him total obedience. This became the new criterion for 'competence'. Now all the other members were required to give the same obedience. Simple. Except that this should have been unthinkable/unacceptable, as indeed it was for the many who left or continued to work under protest. Why should leading members of the organisation who had as much experience as Rajavi himself, submit themselves to only his and his wife's leadership, and only because he declared they should?

Rajavi's ruse was that rather than declare himself as an ordinary leader, he declared himself the ideological leader of the Mojahedin, a new concept in the organisation's structure. Maryam it was said had recognised something in Rajavi that no one else had and that was his unique ideological superiority. This explained her unquestioning devotion to him. Since she had achieved this, so could all the other members by following her example; that is, recognise and accept Rajavi's transcendent ideological qualification to lead the organisation from above with reference to no one but God; which would of itself, demand total obedience to his commands. Again, simple. But this approach allowed Rajavi to bamboozle the members by placing himself in a position beyond criticism.

Rajavi told the ordinary members of the organisation that before the Ideological Revolution, they had acted out of hatred for Khomeini and all that he stood for. This, however, was not ever going to be enough to combat the ideology of Khomeinism. What was needed, he told them, was that they love Rajavi, the embodiment of their ideology, as much as they hated Khomeini. Only in this way would they ever be capable of making the sacrifices necessary for the Mojahedin to succeed in overthrowing the regime. Previous to the Ideological Revolution, the ultimate sacrifice had been for a member or supporter of the Mojahedin to give their life. This now was not enough. It was easy to die in these circumstances. What was needed was for everyone to become a 'living martyr'. That is, to live beyond the mentality of possible death by torture or execution, and to offer their life to Rajavi on a continuing basis to make use of as he deemed necessary, for the sake of the struggle. This would require much greater devotion and suffering than a mere death. This concept of 'living martyr' was also important for Rajavi because he was becoming aware that the recruitment of new members was both limited and difficult. He had to convince ordinary Iranians that they wouldn't be discriminated against because they had no previous history of struggle. What Rajavi wanted were devotees, not heroes.

In this way, Rajavi placed the onus for change on his followers. They not only needed to accept a change of leader, which because they revered Rajavi, they were willing to do, but beyond that Rajavi required that they change themselves. It was a ploy, which suited Rajavi well. Firstly, it made everyone busy wondering what it meant to be a living martyr (no job description was provided!) and whether they lived up to expectations. Secondly, it allowed Rajavi to 'equalise' the status of former political prisoners and those who had had no previous political activity at all. Rajavi needed the energy of both, but he saw that a hierarchy of 'revolutionary sacrifice' was depriving him of the devoted energies of those lower down the scale. Most importantly, it enabled him to have Maryam accepted as co-leader. Rajavi held Maryam up as the example. She had never been seriously in prison or been tortured and yet she was more devoted to the ideology than everyone else, regardless of their past.

This concept changed the organisational structure profoundly. It meant that people could no longer prove themselves in clearly observable ways, such as their resistance to torture, or even how much knowledge they had. They now had to discover what Rajavi meant by ideological devotion and act accordingly. It soon became apparent for those who had close observation of Maryam, that what was required, was simply unquestioning obedience.

About the beginnings of cult culture

The organisation, which Rajavi inherited outside Iran, was different from that which operated inside the country. In essence Reza Raisi had created it with his unique and personal interpretation of the original ethos of the Mojahedin. The Mojahedin supporters outside Iran were largely educated, middle class and from wealthy, often influential, families. Raisi brought them up to think politically and to act on principle. For Rajavi, however, this did not suit his purpose at all. He didn't want his followers to think politically since this might lead them to question his decisions. Neither did he want them to act on principle, because this would hamper his mercenary ambitions.

Rajavi set about manipulating the members' idealism and readiness for self-sacrifice to suit his own needs. He pushed the members to work harder and not to ask questions. He changed the ethos of the organisation by passing messages down to the membership of what he expected of them. The major theme of the time was that 'ideology is what you do, not what you say'. In other words, don't speak, act. He charged the members emotionally with a diet of horror – that created by Khomeini inside Iran, and of hope – that offered by Rajavi outside Iran. By the time he announced the Ideological Revolution, he had already transformed his supporters into a highly disciplined force, ready to act on his command. Now he had to set about changing their minds, or rather, numbing their minds, so those small matters such as politics, ideology or principle would not hinder or interfere with this discipline. He shifted the benchmark for devotion from discipline to obedience, a subtle, but highly significant change. It became necessary for anyone joining the Mojahedin to first accept that they were entering a pyramid system, in which all the decisions came from the very top.

From the beginning of his association with the Mojahedin, Rajavi had been a voracious reader. He read everything he could on politics, philosophy and psychology. Using the mishmash of knowledge he assimilated from this reading, he began to emulate the tactics of Mao in the inculcation of the Mojahedin membership. The foremost necessity was to establish his own unrivalled and absolute leadership over the whole organisation. With the Ideological Revolution, he achieved this and was able to make it public on 8th February 1985. Once in this role, he could more easily manipulate the members.

Most probably Rajavi didn't set out to create a cult. But the methods he chose to employ show all the classic characteristics of cult inculcation. Some of the more important ones are described here. It should be noted that once these methods are introduced, they take on a life of their own, and become reinforced by the membership as they try to make sense of the unreality, which is created. There is no referent but Rajavi and he deliberately keeps himself and his ideas mysterious and unclear.

Neshasts (Meetings)

Meetings are the mainstays for Rajavi as his means of indoctrination. Through the means of meetings, he is able to send his ideological messages into the hearts of all the members. First he starts by speaking personally to three or four hand picked people and gives them hints on what he expects from them. He then sends them away to think. He brings them back into these small, discrete meetings, again and again until they come back with matching stories. Then in a bigger meeting of ten or twenty people, he does the same thing using the first three or four people to speak and create the example, while requiring that the others catch up with them. This works because for the second group of people, the first people seem to be more ideologically aware and tuned in since they are talking about things that the others have no clue about and have never heard of.

These secondary meetings go on as the first, until these further twenty people are 'cooked'. Rajavi notes the contribution of these individuals and their stories, plus all the reports that they have been made to write. This pattern is repeated and grows up to the big meeting. By this time, some more hints have been given out through these twenty people to all the ordinary members, who after the big general meeting, are then expected to come out with their own stories of how they have understood the new ideological development. After that comes the time for a reshuffle in the organisation so that those who have shown themselves most loyal are promoted – until the next time.

The meetings after Forouq-e Javidan (Rajavi's failed military coup of 1988, and his second bid for power) were no different, except that after suffering such losses and emotional damage, the members were more willingly looking for some justification which would allow them to be forgiven by their ideological leader. This was in the hope that if they could get past this phase, the next time would give them a victory. It is taboo to even think about blaming the ideological leader, even in your mind.

Daily Reports

Since the Ideological Revolution in 1985, Rajavi has sought to impose more and more control over members. Beyond the organisational discipline there emerged a mental and spiritual discipline that had little to do with the task at hand. A basic requirement of all members was to write a daily report. This was not just to report what work a person had done or the problems they had encountered performing their duties. It was also a requirement that the members wrote about their relations with other people, quarrels they had or disagreements about any issues, or even whether people had a particular friendship with one another. This ostensibly allowed the responsible person to progress work, resolve conflicts and put right people's erroneous ideas or misconceptions. As a simple example, a person might write that a colleague had spoken angrily toward them and that they had been offended. The person in charge might then call them into a meeting in which the first person could explain that they were angry because of something unrelated to the issue at hand. They would then apologise to the other colleague and resolve to deal better with their angry feelings.

However, these daily reports gave much more information than the writers intended or knew. It showed the weaknesses and strengths and points of resistance or capitulation of individuals, both the writers and those who were written about. This allowed the massuls (those in charge) to use the most suitable psychological methods by which to manipulate members.

However, these instructions to manipulate, always came from the very top. A massul who received a report about which they had doubts as to how they should handle the information, would always pass this information on to their own massul and so forth. Any answer would come from above and be passed down to the relevant level. This is where the original organisational discipline instilled in members from the beginning of the struggle was used, and which had been necessary to protect the members and the organisation from its enemies.

Members were happy to exist in a hierarchy of command, so that they never allowed themselves to take a decision on their own behalf, or to deal with someone in a way they personally deemed appropriate. They always referred problems to someone higher up the command, who had more ideological competence than they did. This was fine as long as the problem was about work or methodology etc, but it soon began to be about the thought processes of the individual and whether they were thinking correctly. Not only about their work and activities, but also about their place in the organisation and in particular about their relationship toward the leader.

The major change too was in what was meant by ideological competence. In the original Mojahedin organisation this meant someone who had political, social and moral knowledge and experience. Someone who had undergone ideological instruction as had the first members way back in the 1960s. Since the Ideological Revolution, however, it came to mean someone who is, more than others, unquestioningly obedient to Rajavi, with no ability or desire to think for themselves, who will suppress any previous knowledge or experience they had in order to parrot what Rajavi requires of them.

The daily reports are part of the hold Rajavi has over his membership. If people express dissent or disaffection with the organisation, the information in the reports can often be used to blackmail someone into silence. As the membership has widened to include anyone who would obey Rajavi, people have written about past crimes, drug addiction, wife beating, and child abuse or about strange sexual fantasies, and are afraid of these things being made public.

Daily reports have been used during every phase of the imposition of the Ideological Revolution. For example, a person would be arbitrarily demoted at some point and sent away just to write reports about themselves and to question themselves as to why they were demoted. This would be continued in meetings in which the person would be questioned publicly and humiliated. The purpose is to unbalance the person's critical abilities to the point that they would write anything that has been suggested to them, including any lies about themselves. These papers are required to be signed by the individual and are then kept for future reference.

Later, in a neshast, the person is given hints as to what to write in their reports, and when they submit the report they should imply that now they have 'got it', i.e. grasped the message, and passed the phase. They then undergo extensive video and meeting sessions, during which they must speak in public to the other members about their ideological mistakes and how they have betrayed the leader. How they have now eliminated these erroneous thoughts from their mind, and in their place, cemented in the new understanding.

Isolation

One of the most effective methods used by all cults is to encourage the membership to cut off all contact with the outside world and with other people, so that the only information that the person receives is from within the organisation.

Before the Ideological Revolution, members were actively encouraged to contact their families and friends as a means of extracting money and support from them. Families which expressed their opposition, should be rejected by the member as having sympathy with the regime – even where this was patently untrue. After 1985, this ethos still held true, as long as families could be of benefit to the organisation or perhaps be recruited, then contact was permitted, even required. However, members were also encouraged to believe that contact with their family would corrupt and demean them because these were ordinary people and couldn't possibly understand the true meaning of the revolutionary struggle; families were looking at the issue emotionally rather than rationally and therefore shouldn't be listened to.

This extreme idea was widened to cover the outside world in general. Newspapers and media couldn't be trusted because they were all biased. The British Broadcasting Corporation was referred to as the 'Ayatollah BBC' because it would not grant the Mojahedin editorial control over interviews it held with them. This resentment was further exacerbated when the BBC began to report the changes which were occurring in Iran over the years. In the same way the BBC's John Simpson was also dubbed Ayatollah Simpson because he had interviewed Khomeini on the plane in which he travelled to Iran in February 1979. Simply the fact of such an interview was enough to condemn him in the eyes of the Mojahedin as an apologist for the regime and all its actions. Amnesty International, because it didn't respond to all the Mojahedin's 'exposures' of the crimes of the regime, was biased.

Up to a certain point, Rajavi didn't need to create this isolation in a particular way. It is a common theme among extreme groups that they see themselves as different from the rest of humanity and as possessing a unique and superior understanding of the realities of life. However, as Rajavi's role in the Mojahedin became more and more defined as the ideological leader, it became more important for him to create a kind of internal isolation within the organisation too. In this way, criticism and analysis did not take root and allow a faction to grow against him or to challenge his leadership.

All outside contact was cut. The reason given was that members were being protected from the corrupt world, when their access to families, friends, radio, newspapers, and even books was denied them. No member could have any money, passport or other identification documents. Any helping hand, any possible ties with those outside, were cut. The later separation of spouses and children further added to this isolation. Those who were in Iraq were left completely isolated. But there were many that still worked and travelled in the West undertaking political activities. How could they be isolated?

This is where the psychology of internal isolation was really put to use. From the beginning of the organisation there developed a culture of overwork. People 'proved' their devotion by working impossibly long hours, even to the extent of going without sleep for days at a time. This was continued, even when it became obvious to all involved, that in fact less was being achieved by such exhausted people as could have been achieved had everyone worked on a shift rota and had eight hours sleep each day. The chronic fatigue of members served to disorientate them and dull their capacity to think. This suited Rajavi very well.

In addition to this, he devised a system by which members were moved from place to place regularly, whether inside Iraq or abroad. People lived out of a small suitcase and changed their place often. People's responsibilities were changed regularly and frequently, and they were not allowed to stay in one job for any length of time. This meant that people didn't work together for long, so that even where a person did undertake a single task for several years, the people around them, and in particular their massul, changed frequently. No friendships were allowed to build up between members, although people had known one another for years and an intrinsic trust existed between all members as if they were all 'family'.

People were not left in highly exposed positions such as being the organisation's representative in a country, for very long. This would give the person too much power. But promotion and demotion was also part of the plan to disorientate members. Praise and criticism would be used to manipulate a person's thoughts. Those who expressed doubt or showed unwillingness were demoted and criticised, often publicly to act as a lesson for others.

All in all, this policy of isolation means that members find it extremely hard to string a coherent thought together, let alone critically analyse their current situation. The knowledge too that other people might report your behaviour or speech in a daily report adds to this inability for the person to think properly about anything.

It is very hard to test an idea without a 'mirror' to bounce it off. When an idea is kept revolving round and round in a person's own mind and the prevailing external message conveys the opposite meaning to the one the person is gaining, this is truly disorientating and debilitating. That this has led to the mental breakdown of several members is hardly surprising. Many of those affected are highly intelligent, highly educated people, whose minds are now expected to atrophy at the behest of the leader. How can this be achieved without damage?

The culture within the Mojahedin of not sleeping originally arose from the need for more work to be done than there were people to do it. Those who had risen in the organisation and were able to be given more responsibility, were not as many as the amount of work which needed to be done. Rajavi simply exploited this willingness to sacrifice their health and well being for his own ends.

Devotion to the Leader

As a complementary part of the concept of isolation, love of the leader is used to 'fill the gap'. Helplessness and hopelessness are encouraged. The prevailing ethos is that you are nothing and can do nothing. You owe everything to Rajavi and will collapse and fail without his guidance. If you leave the Mojahedin, you will quickly become corrupted and end up as a prostitute or drug addict or a murderer. The only key to survival and a decent life is to give complete obedience to Rajavi (via Maryam). You are evil unless you follow Rajavi, and you must remind yourself of this every day, write it in your daily report and say it in every neshast. The purpose of this is to safeguard the rights of the leader and not let any individualism creep in. If you have your own thoughts or feelings, you are stealing from the leader. Your body and mind belongs to the leader, not to the individual. Only he can use it for good, you will use it for evil.

The basic concept that governs the organisation is that every moment a person spends for the leader, whether in thought or in deed, is spent for good, and every other moment, even when you are asleep or believe you are doing good, is spent in favour of evil. You do not have the right to decide what is good, only Rajavi can do this. If you help other people using your own decisions you are helping evil. Yet if you kill and bomb and maim people on 'Massoud and Maryam's legs' you are doing good.

After some time, this becomes a way of life and members become comfortable in this atmosphere. In fact they lose their volition and become irresponsible like a child. They are responsible to the leader only and he is responsible for good and bad and making every decision. Even in religious belief, they are only questioned in respect of how much they have followed the leader. Members will not be responsible before God for Rajavi's mistakes. He has sacrificed himself and taken the blame so that they will be free. (This, of course, has echoes of the role of Jesus Christ in the Christian faith, but this is not Rajavi's intention or meaning at all.)

All these methods not only confuse and disempower people, but they also isolate people. You can never be sure of doing the right thing; you must always doubt yourself. Members are instructed not to compare themselves with others and only to use the leader as a guide to their behaviour. Again this breaks down the connections between people and denies them a 'society' within which to fit. There is total trust between all the members of the Mojahedin, as a group of people facing an outside enemy (the rest of the corrupting world) they must trust one another completely. But, there is also a total absence of trust between all the members because no one can ever be sure what anyone else is really thinking, or even what oneself is thinking and therefore it is easy to lose trust in oneself as a rational being. The only certainty that remains is to listen to and obey Rajavi.

When Rajavi made himself sole leader and elevated himself to the point where he is now, it is certain that he hadn't the intention of creating a cult from the organisation. He merely used the organisation for his own aggrandisement in order to be in a position to seize power more totally. And yet, it is a cult, and exists as one in an organic sense. A cult takes on a life of its own and follows its own dynamic. Once Rajavi instigated the changes in the organisation, these changes took on a dynamic life of their own as they are filtered down the ranks and met with all the various individuals who make up the membership. It is inevitable that people interpret and act out these changes in as many ways as there are people involved and that this is out of the range of all Rajavi's planning and control. The more extreme the interpretation, the more corrupting that is of the person and thereby the environment around that person.

Ideological indoctrination and psychological manipulation

These are the two methods by which Rajavi has imposed his control over the organisation, and are the cornerstones underpinning all cult activities. All activities in the Mojahedin are group activities. No one is left to work, rest, eat or sleep alone. And this community life enables Rajavi to foist the most outlandish ideas onto people. This is because of the 'example of others' principle or 'peer pressure' whereby if you see that everyone else is conforming then you do so too. It is also because of the system of daily reports and daily neshasts in which people report on one another and themselves, and so a certain degree of conformity is necessary just to survive. Yet there is no 'society' in the organisation, no one enjoys friendships or relationships with anyone other than the leaders. Sitting and chatting is scorned as the base behaviour which only supporters indulge in through their ignorance. Indeed, when the massuls do sit and talk, it is precisely to denigrate the supporters as lesser, weaker human beings.

When Rajavi addresses his closed and captive audience and presents them with the latest in his ideological twists and turns, he is addressing a willing audience. People want to accept what he says because they believe in the Mojahedin and they believe in his leadership. So, there is a willingness to accept whatever is being told them. Those who question or do not understand what is being said, are often willing to believe that this is because they haven't the capacity to understand and that they need guidance and enlightenment. This is provided through local neshasts with the massul or other competent people. Every individual in the organisation has their own profile, built up from the information contained in their reports. When required, this profile is used as the basis for individual guidance. That is, the person's strengths and weaknesses are manipulated until they come around to the correct way of thinking.

Rajavi's explanations are vague and swathed in mythological religious references. The second phase of the Ideological Revolution, the so-called, 'Internal Revolution' in 1989, for example, was introduced during a five-day neshast, which was exactly that, five days of Rajavi addressing the membership in Iraq. Rajavi took five days to introduce and explain his simple requirement, which was, 'divorce your spouse, divest yourself of sexuality and devote your undivided self to me'.

This five-day neshast is shown to those newly involved in the organisation, that is, the refugees who are recruited as supporters in the West. Once a person shows enough capacity to be fooled, they are flattered by being told that they are ready to understand what Rajavi requires. However, the video is only shown in the same environment as the actual meeting was held.

That is, over five days, in a dark enclosed room, without adequate breaks and when the persons watching are tired and vulnerable. Where possible, the massul then works with this person intensively in order to inculcate the ideas more deeply into their mind.

The person is semi-isolated and treated with a degree of kindness and affection which is not offered to others. With careful treatment and attention, the person is lulled into a false sense of security and soon reveals to the massul, their innermost thoughts and feelings. From this, the leadership can extract the person's weaknesses and possible points of resistance to the ideology. The weaknesses are usually expressed as needs, and most refugees are needy not of food and shelter, important as these are, but of contact with same language speakers, people of the same culture, and needy of support, love and affection. Even families, where it might be expected that they could offer one another this love and affection, while struggling to survive as refugees, are often under severe strain and cannot always support one another.

The Mojahedin know this and offer them a safe haven and reinforce their cultural background and the need for social contact. Parties, celebrations, and all these activities are part of the organisation's efforts to reproduce the Iranian cultural and social atmosphere for which refugees are most homesick. Although the ideology has required members of the Mojahedin to separate from their spouse and children, families and particularly children are welcomed into the organisation's Western bases. It is this kindness and warmth, which draws the new people in. An atmosphere of uncritical support taps into the weaknesses and needs of vulnerable people.

Since the 1989/90, second phase of the Ideological Revolution, those who have joined as supporters of the Mojahedin, have mostly been uneducated refugees from Iran. They have either been supporters of the Mojahedin inside the country and have just managed to escape, or they are young people who have escaped because they see no future for themselves in Iran. Usually they don't yet have the knowledge or opportunity to work out a better future for themselves in the

West. They see the existing Iranian community in the West as completely out of touch with their country and strangely complacent about its past sufferings and its future. For a young person having undergone the hardship of growing up under severe restrictions, repression and war, this can act as a fire to light the fuse of their anger and passion. This is exactly what the Mojahedin want and need in order to sweep this person's mind off its feet and indoctrinate them with the Mojahedin's ideology.

Those who are already established in the West and/or are educated, but still join, are often running away from another problem. An example of this was a man from the north of England who with his English wife, had three children and ran a successful sandwich shop. He wanted to escape his wife and current lifestyle, so he put the house and business in his wife's name and simply disappeared off to Iraq to join the army. Whatever protest or resistance his wife raised was quashed, not by the husband, but by the women massuls in London. It was they who refused the wife access or argument on the grounds that she was preventing her husband from fulfilling his true calling in life. Her, and their children's rights, were trampled upon by other women who otherwise purported to be 'free' of male domination.

A different problem that many spouses, mostly women, suffered came after the Forouq-e Javidan operation when the Mojahedin refused to issue any death certificates. They found it impossible to prove that their husband or wife had died and that they were left the estate. So, for example, where a mortgage on a property was in joint names, the spouse couldn't sell it or redeem the mortgage or even claim social security without the spouse's co-signature. This also arose as a problem when one spouse agreed to divorce and the other didn't. These divorces were not legal and have no legal status. So, if one spouse left and arrived in the West to seek asylum, they also experienced difficulties over custody of children and control of property. It also meant that they couldn't marry again. One man who had married in Iran, but had been naturalised in Britain and had British citizenship solved this. His wife remained in the Mojahedin, but he could not remarry in Britain where his marriage was legally recognised, as he had no divorce settlement. So he fled to Sweden and claimed asylum there so that he could marry again in Sweden.

Indoctrination is performed both communally en masse, and on a more personal level, depending on the propensity of any one individual. Videos are shown to people according to the areas of doubt or criticism. These are used to impress the person with the might and success of the Mojahedin throughout its history. Rajavi is portrayed as a kind of stern, but avuncular, almost mythical charismatic character. He is portrayed as having a superior level of understanding, which he deigns out of love for humanity to share with the lesser beings of the Mojahedin. The rest of the world are of course, lost souls and couldn't possibly even begin to understand. So, Rajavi is doing everyone a great honour by considering them worthy enough to share a little of his great vision and wisdom.

Most people respond positively to this flattery even though it is unreal; that is, it has no basis in what is really true. The Mojahedin make their own reality and live it out for themselves. They will allow themselves to be indoctrinated because that is the only way they can continue to make sense of the anathema that the organisation has become in the Iranian political scene. The twist is that the rest of the world is wrong and only Rajavi and by implication, his followers, are right. So, they continue convincing themselves that Rajavi is right.

The psychological manipulation of members springs from Rajavi's avid interest in using psychology as a means of controlling people. He has read voraciously from the time that he left prison, books on politics, psychology and history etc. His ideology is a mishmash of all these books, and not a single part of it derives from original thinking. Rajavi uses psychological manipulation to control people. The massuls are instructed to behave in particular ways towards individuals according to what is required of them or in response to a problem they might have. On a simple level, the warmth and affection shown to newcomers is a basic method of attracting them, fulfilling a basic need, which they lack. The person is told – and this is the ideological element – that if they look for love and affection outside Maryam they will become corrupt and 'nothing', they will be condemned to a life of obscurity, drudgery and meaninglessness. A picture of ordinary married life is portrayed as a hellish prison for both sexes. Children are the ultimate burden, removing the person further and further from the glorious joy and happiness that could be theirs if they give all their love to Maryam. She will return their love a hundred fold, and only inside the Mojahedin they will be able to fulfil their true potential as a human being.

Once a person is inside the organisation and has cut their links with the outside world, the manipulation becomes both more complex and at the same time, easier. It is easier because the person is deprived of any external reference point to test out the validity of their perception. They can only accept that what is happening to them and being said to them, is a true representation of life. So, if, one day, everyone around them suddenly decides to ignore them, they will accept a self-explanation that they have done something wrong and will try to make amends so that they are acceptable again. If the person questions or objects to the behaviour of others toward them, their perceptions are dismissed as fantasy. The other people, the member is informed, are busy working all out for Rajavi and the member himself, should work harder and not think about what others are doing. So, the member begins to accept that their perception of reality is somehow wrong and they try to adjust their thoughts according to the analysis of their massul. That is that the problem must lie in the individual himself and that the only solution is to work harder and not to think. After a while a person can find a very comfortable existence like this.

Later Rajavi used the public perception of his marriage to Maryam as scandalous, to test and break the members. In a way it was a sacrifice that he allowed himself to be judged so that the members who could accept that for the ideological leader nothing is a sin, would be freed from sexism. Of course, it has always been emphasised that this only applies to the leader and nobody else. Rajavi thought that the ones who accepted this would be thoroughly devoted to him, but he later found that he had to separate families as well as concentrate on their thoughts and minds. Of course this works for some time because if you accept this you feel a relief and some sort of personal irresponsibility. The problem is that it does not last long and every now and then you will need another injection of this dose. That is why the Ideological Revolution of Rajavi has never ended and as Maryam Rajavi puts it, 'You do not know how much you have to give. You think you have given what you had but I know what you have and I will get all of this out of you for the revolution' (i.e. Rajavi)

Chapter 9

ARMED STRUGGLE

Inside Iran, the Mojahedin, right up to and for some time after the Ideological Revolution, maintained their strong popular support. This support was not fuelled by people's devotion to Rajavi. It was simply a result of the severity of the regime's repression and the need to join or support a strong, proven resistance movement. Many, many ordinary people were willing to put themselves at extreme risk to provide succour and support for the Mojahedin's guerrilla units. These members were directly fighting against Khomeini's repressive forces; that is, the officials and employees, the ideological supporters and campaigners for the Khomeini regime.

Before 1986 when the French asked Rajavi to leave Paris and he removed his headquarters to Iraq, the Mojahedin had already used all their resources inside Iran. In order to continue their armed struggle they started using their remaining militia in motorcycle teams which attacked governmental buildings and Pasdaran patrols. During a strategy meeting in the mid 1980s, Rajavi announced that if they only achieve the death of seven Pasdaran every week, the regime would be toppled, the so-called seven-sevenths strategy. But they never achieved this target and eventually the strategy died. Rajavi then intensified his strategy of attaching himself more and more to Saddam Hussein. (Remember Rajavi and his outfit were mostly in Paris at this time.)

When the Ideological Revolution was announced in 1985, the guerrilla fighters were led by Ali Zarkesh. Upon hearing these changes, Zarkesh dismissed the Ideological Revolution and refused to recognise Rajavi's new self-proclaimed role as well as that of his wife. As far as Zarkesh was concerned, there was no place for such individualism in the organisation. The Mojahedin were fighting one of the most suppressive regimes in the world's recent history. Those inside Iran were having a desperate time of it and hadn't the luxury of playing power games within the organisation. They were daily risking life and limb to carry out the Mojahedin's original aim, which was to break the atmosphere of repression by fighting back against and thereby exposing, the weaknesses of Khomeini's suppressive forces. They were stoically pursuing Rajavi's own seven-sevenths policy with few resources and little in the way of success.

Rajavi's meddling with the organisation's leadership threw the internal armed struggle into disarray. No one was certain anymore who the leaders were or what the Mojahedin's new ideology meant. Prisoners in particular, barely surviving in the dire conditions and frequently subjected to torture, felt they had been betrayed. At first, many didn't believe what the prison guards gleefully told them about Rajavi's marriage to Abrishamchi's wife. Once they realised that it was true, many became disaffected and gave up their support for the Mojahedin. Isolated and under severe hardship, they only had their faith in the Mojahedin's unbending struggle to help them withstand years of imprisonment. Rajavi's actions cast doubt for them on the organisation's future and its commitment to them.

In Paris, Rajavi was in contact with Zarkesh and other isolated operational cells, by telephone. Rajavi knew that he couldn't leave Zarkesh in command inside Iran. Zarkesh's refusal to accept his leadership would lead him eventually to take control of the organisation there and denounce Rajavi as a traitor. This split in the organisation would leave Rajavi isolated outside the country, robbing him of all the martyrs he needed to bolster his own position. So Rajavi tricked Zarkesh into making the perilous journey out of Iran to visit him in Paris. Once in

Paris, Zarkesh was immediately subjected to Rajavi's wrath. He was humiliated, scorned and finally demoted to the level of private in the new army, the National Liberation Army. Zarkesh remained loyal to the Mojahedin's struggle until the end of his life, but never accepted Rajavi's role as ideological leader.

With Zarkesh in Paris, Iran was left without a commander. Once the NLA was formed in 1987, Rajavi appointed Maryam as commander of the armed struggle in Iran. She never even attempted to do the job. The reason quickly became clear when Rajavi made a surprising announcement. He told the Mojahedin members inside Iran that they should all make their way out of the country to the bases in Iraqi Kurdistan. There they would be trained and briefed and sent back into Iran to perform operations against the regime. Rajavi declared that anyone who stayed inside Iran was no longer with the Mojahedin and any activities they were involved in were not acceptable to the Mojahedin. At the same time it should be noted that in practice, the Mojahedin continued to claim any martyrs or prisoners as their own in complete disregard of this statement.

Rajavi's demand was strange. He had the ability to control the cells from Paris, so why would he want to take people, at great risk, out of Iran and out of the struggle? The answer lay in the nature of Rajavi's new role as ideological leader. This was so alien to the original concept of the Mojahedin's founders that he had to foist it upon the members by means of psychological manipulation. Anyone beyond the sphere of manipulation would not be able to accept or submit to Rajavi's leadership simply because it really had nothing to do with the issue at hand, which was confronting and toppling the Khomeini regime.

Rajavi knew that if members stayed in Iran out of his reach, they would leave and not obey him. Even worse, they might declare an independent Mojahedin organisation inside Iran. They, like all the other members, had to be within the sphere of manipulation. Faced with the potential split of the organisation, he announced that everyone in Iran had to leave and join the army in Iraq. Once inside the atmosphere of the cult, Rajavi could make them believe in his leadership.

Relationship of Mojahedin with Iraq

Also, outside Iran, Rajavi had been making his own, separate, plans for the armed struggle. He had seen an opportunity in neighbouring Iraq, which was at war with Iran, to create an ally for the Mojahedin's activities.

The Kurdish Democratic Party had joined the NCRI on the Mojahedin's invitation. It soon became apparent what use Rajavi had for the organisation. Rajavi used the Kurdish Democratic Party of Iran to initiate and develop his contacts with Iraqi leaders. The KDP had more open relations with Iraq. For the Mojahedin, accepting their leader Ghasemlou into the NCRI was a means to develop this covert relationship with Iraq under the cover of the KDP. Once Rajavi had secured his relationship directly with Iraq and had no further need for them, he ousted the KDP from the NCRI.

Between 1980 and 1988, Iraq was the aggressor in a full-scale war with Iran. It was a hugely damaging war in which the Iraqis used chemical weapons against Iranian soldiers. This war profoundly influenced the Iranian people's perception of the Mojahedin's activities and served to alienate them ever more. The people suffered a double burden; that of Khomeini's internal repression and of a dangerous all-consuming war. The people of Iran were not in a situation to look kindly or sympathetically on the Mojahedin's armed incursions from Iraqi territory against the forces, which were protecting Iran from invasion. It appeared as though the Mojahedin were actually helping Iraq in its war against Iran, whether intentionally or not.

In 1983, before establishing bases in Iraq, Rajavi had signed a peace agreement with Saddam and announced that peace was possible with Iraq and that is was only the Iranian regime which wanted to continue the war! He announced that peace would spell the end of the Iranian regime and victory for the Mojahedin. Many politicians warned him that in the long run, by making this agreement, he would allow himself to become a bargaining chip for Saddam. Now, nearly fifteen years after the war ended, it seems they were right. The Mojahedin are inextricably linked with and beholden to Saddam. He plays them as a card in his negotiations with Iran. It is Saddam

Hussein who dictates whether the Mojahedin can cross the border into Iran or not, and he does this only with his own interests in mind.

Since 1983, the Mojahedin had established bases in Iranian Kurdistan, as previously had the Fedayeen and others before them. In addition to the urban guerrilla warfare which was being continued in conditions of extreme danger by the members and supporters still left inside Iran, the Mojahedin were also launching attacks on the regime's forces who were fighting the Iraqis. The targets were the ideologically motivated Pasdaran and Revolutionary Guards, rather than the regular army. But the attacks were made on forces fighting the country's enemy. Not many Iranians wished to see the Iraqis overrun their country no matter how hated Khomeini's rule was.

In a matter of only two years, the Mojahedin were pushed back from Iranian Kurdistan by the Pasdaran, and were forced to take refuge in Iraqi Kurdistan. The Mojahedin had maintained a covert relationship with Iraq since 1983, having representatives there and exchanging information and intelligence, and using Iraq for their backup in Kurdistan. So this fallback was not problematic for them.

For the international community, the unspoken agenda was now that Iraq and the Mojahedin could work together with the backing of the West, to topple the Khomeini regime. The Mojahedin (or in the Western mind, the NCRI) would then be a ready replacement in Iran and it would all have a good ending. The West had little idea at this time of the ruthless nature of either Saddam Hussein or of Rajavi and his intentions. Could these two, the dictator and the autocrat, have succeeded? It is impossible to say. Would Saddam have killed Rajavi and invaded parts of Iran? Would Rajavi have killed other members of the NCRI in order to take power in Iran, and become the new Khomeini in Iran? Would they share their programme of building weapons of mass destruction and become a united force against Kuwait or even Israel? None of this came to pass, but the two men are still hand in hand.

For the time being, the international political community backed them both. The West had armed Saddam Hussein against Iran and saw the Mojahedin as part of their ambitions to oust the Khomeini regime and replace it with a compliant, grateful Mojahedin. At that time the NCRI was put forward as the instrument for achieving power in Iran with a six month interim government to be established after the fall of the Khomeini regime. However, in 1986, the Mojahedin's host government France, asked Rajavi to leave the country. The Mojahedin claim that France did this because they were getting close to regime. If this is so, then it simply means that France had given up on the Mojahedin and saw they were wasting their money. At the same time, France had good relations with Iraq and by having the Mojahedin in Iraq they could still 'support' them while at the same time, by having them work with Saddam there was more chance of success in changing the regime in Iran.

It is possible that the Mojahedin would have gone anyway because they were building good relations with Iraq from 1983, and their armed struggle was being waged from there. Having France ask them to leave was simply an excuse for them to go, although they tried to portray it as their choice anyway. Rajavi introduced the move to Iraq to the organisation's members as his decision and part of his strategy for the imminent overthrow.

In June 1986, Rajavi moved his headquarters to Iraq with the agreement of Saddam Hussein. This move was bound to attract controversy in the Iranian political community and in Iranian public opinion. When going to Iraq, Rajavi announced that the departure of the Mojahedin from the West ended the legitimacy for every refugee for staying in the West. The logic behind this was that the refugees only had legitimacy because of the Mojahedin's fight against the regime. In this way, Rajavi hoped to bully more people into joining his organisation. Naturally, this did not go down well with the refugees who had fled Iran because of the horrific human rights violations and mass suppression, rather than because of anything the Mojahedin had done or claimed. The perception of many, right or wrong, was that the Mojahedin were actually prolonging the repression because of the extreme threat they posed to the regime, particularly with the war.

Rajavi's announcement sprang from the belief, which he held from the beginning of the revolution in which he saw himself as the equivalent of Khomeini. He had the ambition even at the beginning of the revolution, before he came to Paris, to be the leader of the Muslim world, not just Iran. Today, Rajavi is no longer a political leader for his supporters and the Mojahedin, although they see Iran as the first step in their plans. The ideology is global and the aim is international domination. As explained elsewhere, Rajavi is following Mao step by step, in his own Muslim version.

Khomeini recognised this ambition back in 1979 when he said 'the boy calls himself the leader'. So Rajavi's fight with Khomeini was significant from an ideological point of view, from the start. Once Khomeini died, Rajavi continued to fight the 'Khomeini regime' even though the religious leader of the country was Khamenei and the elected President was Rafsanjani. If Rajavi had changed his fight to be against these two, then he would have lessened his own position since neither of these men had the qualification, credibility or the popular support of Khomeini. This began to be a problem quite quickly after Khomeini died. The world trailed off its use of the expression 'Khomeini regime' and began dealing with reality. The leadership of Iran fairly soon looked far more diffuse. Rajavi couldn't continue to oppose someone who was dead and the prevailing ethos of the country was gradually changing. Elections were being held, the grip on power was being forced into more, divergent hands. It became clear to everyone that the regime was 'established' and had begun to mature and that the likelihood of a counter-revolution at least from outside, was receding rapidly year by year. This finally came to a head when President Mohammad Khatami was elected with millions of votes. It could no longer be claimed that the reactionaries had total control.

So Rajavi was left more and more isolated in his position. The Mojahedin tried their best to stop these changes, whether by propaganda or by terrorist activities. Khatami for his part was clever enough not to retaliate against these attacks. In some cases, there has even been direct and indirect co-operation with

the hardliners in Iran who now had a common interest with the
Mojahedin in stopping the process of change. There have been
cases of assassinations, such as that of retired General Shirazi,
which were first claimed by the Mojahedin and were later found
to be the work of the hardliner groups in Iran and vice versa.

Is this true?

Formation of the National Liberation Army of Iran in Iraq

The recruitment drive was continuing in the West. When Rajavi
moved to Iraq, the organisation began sending all its recruits
there for guerrilla training. During February and March 1987 a
wave of armed resistance activities were launched from inside
Iraqi territory. Shortly afterwards, in June 1987, the National
Liberation Army was founded. This transformed the
Mojahedin's armed resistance from a guerrilla force into a
military force. The change obviously came about because of
increased resources. That is, Rajavi accepted military facilities,
training and arms from Saddam Hussein.

The effect of this army on the armed struggle was initially
positive. The attacks on Iran were far more serious and
successful, in that fewer Mojahedin were being killed. However,
it also meant that the armed struggle was now based not on the
activities of the members inside Iran, but rather on an external
armed force, outside Iranian borders and out of touch with
ordinary Iranian people.

Maryam was named Deputy Commander in Chief of the
National Liberation Army. This gave her a higher position than
even the most experienced military members. (Some members
had been fairly high ranking officers in Iran's military before
the revolution.) What reaction did this evoke? On one hand it
isn't necessary for an executive head of something to be an
expert in the field of operations. Maryam, like any other CEO,
was able to consult the military experts and then impose a new
way of doing things. In fact, the leadership of Maryam did a lot
to help women, even from the point of view of having uniforms,
which allowed them more physical freedom. Organising
sanitary facilities for women, providing childcare and schools
(when they were still allowed to keep their children!) freed the

women to concentrate on their work. However, breaking the mental barriers that women still had came later.

This is something, which was a positive aspect of Rajavi's leadership, changing the role and mentality of women, and perhaps only women can really appreciate its impact and implications. Yet Rajavi was doing this for his own benefit, to break down the family ties and get everyone to be devoted to him. Rajavi knew well enough that the number of people with him would not increase by any significant amount. The existing members had come because of the revolution and he had now gone too far for anybody from outside to catch up and accept the changes, therefore outsiders were treated differently and not told about every aspect of Rajavi's ideology (not even the NCRI members). Therefore he needed every man and woman to work to their full capacity, that is, to fight. Men did not need this incentive to fight, but women needed an incentive to fight and the men in the organisation needed to accept them.

Rajavi has said that if he had only had enough soldiers to fight for him, he would not have done this before getting to power in Iran. One clear disadvantage for the Iranian regime is its attitude towards women. This of course was something Rajavi could not ignore and had to take advantage of. The dilemma for him is that he wants everything. He wants to use the women's issue and he want to use the Islamic tendencies of the people at the same time. Conflicting guidelines were issued to the members according to which idea was in the ascendant. One year it was okay for women to shake hands with (non-Iranian) men in political meetings, next year it was not. One year propaganda was issued condemning the regime's religious ceremonies like Ashura; next year they did it themselves. Rajavi has this problem in facing the outside world. Inside is another matter. Inside the organisation whatever he says is right. He is the measure of good and bad and the only person responsible for it.

The new army undertook military operations into Iran on a different scale than before. Without doubt, the new military training had an impact on the success of these, in terms of people getting killed or injured, yet no real gains were made.

The idea behind them was still to break the atmosphere of repression inside Iran and to damage the regime's repressive forces. And to prove to their Western sponsors that they could do it. Yet the Mojahedin, while they remained outside the country, could actually make little impact. This is where Rajavi's removal of the organisation's resources out of Iran began to make its negative impact felt.

Even Zarkesh, who was doing as much as he could in Iran, was fooled and brought to Paris. He was demoted and replaced by Maryam who never even attempted to do the job. Then Rajavi announced that anybody who refused to come out and stayed in Iran, was no longer a member. Only coming out and then being sent back from Iraq under instruction to work was valid.

Rajavi never explained why he didn't send some command structure to Iran, but it is now obvious that this would leave the way open to a challenge for leadership of the organisation. At the time of the Iranian revolution in 1979, there were struggles taking place in other countries such as Palestine, Chile, and El Salvador. In each of these struggles, their representatives reflected to the world community what was going on inside their country. With Iran, this was effective for the first few years because the Mojahedin were still active. But Rajavi achieved what the regime itself was failing to do. That is, to destroy the Mojahedin proper inside Iran. He did this by bringing the headquarters outside the country for his own use. No other country's struggle did this. This destroyed the Mojahedin inside Iran. He took all the organisation's resources to Paris, including its leading members who were loyal to him, and he assumed control of the organisation through this. Even if we postulate that Rajavi had to do this after 30th Khordad, he still never tried to rebuild the organisation in Iran. He was afraid it would become something that was beyond his control. It was this same fear that led him to remove Zarkesh.

Rajavi has got to have even the very junior commanders under his personal supervision and change them all the time. Nobody out of his daily reach is allowed to become more than an ordinary soldier for more than six months. Women are useful

[handwritten margin note: Rajavi destroys Mojahedin organisation in Iran?]

93

to Rajavi because they are loyal and don't object to this structure and anyway they couldn't become rivals, not even minor ones. This use of women is something Saddam Hussein is expert in, and Rajavi clearly learned from him.

While the Mojahedin were still in Iran they had potential. But Rajavi destroyed this. The removal to Paris automatically cut the organisation's ties with the people. The new generation of youth in Iran does not know the Mojahedin except as a terrorist group sponsored by Saddam Hussein. For them, Rajavi is a defector and a traitor who has strange ideas about marriage and on the whole the Mojahedin are not something to be interested in. In short, a black page in the history of Iran. Those who knew the Mojahedin and supported their ideas kept their faith, but little by little, people fall away when they see no progress, no contact, and no help from outside. While people were suffering inside Iran with no help, they only saw the marriage, and the removal to Iraq, their national enemy, and they became disillusioned.

Rajavi wanted to be 'the' help, not to garner it from the international community or to form a wider political base which is what the NCRI was supposed to do. Rajavi, from the beginning showed this propensity to overvalue and overestimate himself, putting himself centre stage instead of the people. The primary reason that the mullahs were able to take control in Iran at the time of the revolution was their contact with people all over the country through the mosques. Rajavi failed to take account of the people, relying on his own popularity instead.

The National Liberation Army had a troubled path to tread. Based in Iraq, they were naturally regarded as on enemy territory. Rajavi has never been able to clearly state how he intends to use the NLA in toppling the regime. To imagine that the 10,000 members of this army could confront the Iranian national army was ludicrous. Even Saddam Hussein after years of all out war could not do this. Rajavi vaguely hinted that if the NLA entered Iran at the right time, then the people would spontaneously rise up to support them and they would march on Tehran on a wave of popular support. This means a counter-revolution. Yet, the possibility of this happening was becoming more and more remote as time passed. Rajavi had fewer and fewer grounds for supposing the people of Iran would support the Mojahedin.

Yet as soon as the war with Iraq ended, Rajavi launched a desperate and foolhardy bid for power. He ordered the NLA to attack Iran with disastrous results. The Forouq-e Javidan operation is examined in the next chapter. The point here is that even when they had their chance to do what Rajavi had promised, the NLA failed. Since that time there has been little scope for believing that they could even repeat the exercise let alone succeed. Half the army was killed in the operation. It took years for the members to recover their morale and capacity. Even when they did, Rajavi made a decision in 1991, which was to seal the fate of the NLA and condemn it to little more than a terrorist group.

When Saddam Hussein attacked a neighbouring country for the second time, in 1990, with his invasion of Kuwait, the world was outraged and allied forces attacked Iraq, forcing a withdrawal. In such a climate of worldwide condemnation, the clear strategy for an independent foreign organisation would be to leave Iraq, even on a symbolic level. But Rajavi clearly felt that he had too much to lose and nothing to gain from leaving. Or, even more likely, Saddam would not let him leave without paying a huge price. The Mojahedin stayed. Mojahedin military bases were safe from allied attacks. At that time, no one had any proof to implicate them in complicity with the crimes of Saddam Hussein. It was only afterwards, when the NLA were 'permitted' by Saddam to defend parts of Kurdistan against the Kurdish uprising, that the real nature of the relationship was exposed. The NLA used their tanks and armoured personnel to raze Kurdish villages and kill many of the inhabitants. These were innocent Iraqi Kurds. It became clear that Rajavi was beholden to Iraq such that he would do even this dirty work at their bidding.

Human Rights Watch reported the events and the world discovered an ugly truth behind Rajavi's army. In spite of Mojahedin denials, Rajavi knew he needed to recover ground in the propaganda stakes. He had to again present the NLA as the only force which was actively engaged in and capable of overthrowing the hated regime in Iran.

On 18th October 1991, the NLA held a military parade at Ashraf camp, their main military base in Iraq, as a demonstration of its military strength. Foreign journalists were invited to attend and see for themselves the strength and capacity of the army, which was in reality a small sample of Saddam's weaponry. After Forouq-e Javidan, Iraq had advised Rajavi that there was no possibility for the Mojahedin to attack Iran again in the near future and if the Mojahedin wanted to move forward and make progress in the time available, they would have to be trained. This idea to have the army properly trained was, of course, advertised as Maryam's brilliant idea. Iraq took over and started training, which was mostly Soviet. The Iraqis brought ancient T52 tanks, BMP1 and MTL Russian armoured carriers and other equipment to the Mojahedin camp and taught the Mojahedin how to drive them. Later, small crash courses on security and intelligence, commando fighting and administration courses were held.

For this purpose, they moved some of their own service, repair centres and headquarters into the Mojahedin camp. The Mojahedin became more familiar with real army life as a result and became so much a part of it that it was acceptable for the Iraqi army to communicate with them as a military division. They gave up their amateur transceivers and used proper military equipment. They became familiar with using the basic command and operational terms of the Iraqi army. This, of course, is what enabled the Iraqi army to use the Mojahedin as an instrument to help crush the Kurdish uprising during the Morvarid operation of March 1991.

The military parade of 1991, was the graduation ceremony of this division. In this parade, NLA personnel traversed along a wide purpose built boulevard, passing the observers in the middle. At the end of the street, vehicles were waiting to take the crews of the tanks and other vehicles back to the beginning of the street for them to come down again with more tanks and armoured vehicles. The NLA had acquired a whole army load of equipment from Saddam, but hadn't enough people to show it off, particularly to show women on tanks.

The Gulf War in 1991, proved a testing time for the Mojahedin in many ways. Politically, they estranged themselves from their erstwhile supporters in the West by choosing to remain under Iraqi hegemony. Militarily it was also a disaster. After the war ended, Saddam Hussein saw his opportunity to crush the ensuing Kurdish rebellion in the north of Iraq. The Mojahedin army was also mobilised by Saddam to crush the Kurds. They used their tanks to raze Kurdish villages and kill civilians.

Currently, the Mojahedin have fewer than 5,000 forces in the NLA, and the average age of the organisation's members is nearer fifty than forty years. Rajavi has been desperate in recent years to find younger recruits for the army. His first resort was to recall the children of Mojahedin members who were evacuated in 1991, and many of whom had now grown to be young adults. Their parents were told to demand their children back as a right. Those who were under Mojahedin jurisdiction in the West were quickly returned. Others needed a little more persuasion, but many supporters who had fostered the children, felt duty-bound to return them to their parents, without thinking through the full situation. That is, since the parents had been required previously to reject the children, it was unlikely that Rajavi wanted them now to be reunited with their parents.

The National Liberation Army is now all that remains of the armed struggle to free Iran from its present religious rulers. Having existed outside Iran's borders for so long, they are estranged from the people inside Iran. The only operations they have recently been capable of launching are what amount to terrorist attacks, in which several innocent civilians have been killed and injured. And they are inextricably linked with and beholden to Saddam Hussein, who, regardless of how the rest of the world regards him, Iranians see as their country's erstwhile enemy who used chemical weapons on their army; which the Iranians claim has killed seven thousand men up to the present day. It is Saddam who dictates whether or not the Mojahedin may cross the border into Iran and launch an attack. At present it is not in his interests to do so. He needs to develop better relations with Tehran as part of his attempts to confront American led pressure over his development of weapons of mass destruction.

The Mojahedin as a military force, were finally written off when first the US State Department had them listed as a terrorist entity, then the United Kingdom added them to its list of Proscribed Organisations. Finally, in May 2002, the European Union also listed the Mojahedin as a terrorist entity. It remains to be seen how the Mojahedin respond to a Western attack on Iraq when they are this vulnerable.

Chapter 10

FOREIGN RELATIONS

The Mojahedin needed to have made very different political choices and stances in order to survive and be a real challenge to the regime. Currently their propaganda depicts them as the only alternative to the regime in its entirety. It depicts them as pro-democracy and progressive on the issue of women's rights. But they have in real terms, failed to make the kinds of decisions which would have granted them a future in Iranian politics. Instead, the Mojahedin now finds itself irrelevant in Iran, and even before 11th September, labelled as a terrorist entity by the US and UK governments.

How did this happen? The Mojahedin's political posturing and propaganda hides a very real and fundamental failure. That is, the failure of Rajavi's foreign policy to move away from the politics of 'everything or nothing' and the use of force as the means to achieve it. The depth of failure can be traced through the activities of both the NCRI and the NLA, though its roots are to be found in the Mojahedin's internal relations, through the turning points of the Ideological Revolution and the Internal Revolution.

When Rajavi escaped to France and the Mojahedin was established in the West, the incumbent members, who had mostly been tutored in their Mojahedin identity by Reza Raisi, began actively campaigning for foreign political support. They posed as students, although even from very early on, most were full time revolutionaries who had given up or completed their studies. To add to this image of being students, until the late 1980s, funds and support were still extracted from the Students' Unions of most major educational institutions, wherever people could be persuaded to start a Muslim Iranian Student's Society in their local college, polytechnic or university. So notorious had the Khomeini regime become that this was not difficult to achieve.

The Mojahedin also had the advantage that they had been active and organised among students since before the revolution. This allowed them to move in forcefully and push out the less organised, but no less popular, communist groups. The Mojahedin's expertise in self-propaganda also allowed them to portray themselves as the main opposition. The early attrition of the communist groups' armed forces in Iran by Khomeini, deprived them of the publicity which the Mojahedin's continued operations gave to them. The Mojahedin also made much headway during their anti-liberalism phase in which they actively destroyed the credibility of other Iranian opposition groups and personalities.

The 'diplomacy' section of the Mojahedin was developed from Reza Raisi's framework. Rajavi's methods were more for action and force. He wasn't really interested in talking to anyone except about money, power, arms or land. But fortunately for him there were enough people who had the wisdom to see that Western public and political opinion needed to be courted.

The members who were undertaking this political lobbying were Western educated Iranians from wealthy families, who had enough social niceties and foreign languages, to meet with influential people. Also, the revolutionary atmosphere and the atmosphere in the West coincided.

In the UK, the Conservative victory in the 1979 general election led to a confrontation between employers' interests and the working class represented by the trades unions. The militancy of the time exactly suited the Mojahedin and they found it easy to gain support from all sides, which were in the mood to help 'the oppressed' whoever or wherever they might be. They started at grass roots, visiting the local meetings of various unions and the Constituency Labour Party. Soon they were able to count on a number of loyal and influential supporters in parliament and the political parties, trades unions and various NGOs.

As the contact with politicians and the media developed and now that the anti-liberalism phase had been superseded by the imperatives of the Ideological Revolution it became clear to Rajavi that the revolutionary image of the Mojahedin needed to be hidden. A new glossy image needed to be portrayed to the West in order to maintain support. Their publications developed from *'News on Iran'* into the *'NLA Quarterly'* and *'NCR'*. This made it easier to distance their relationship with Saddam Hussein in Western eyes, while maintaining the glamorous image of their armed struggle as being led by women and operated independently and courageously from just over the Iranian border.

Up to the failed Forouq-e Javidan operation in 1988, the Mojahedin was enjoying some degree of success and popularity. The regime was exerting its most repressive measures; the atrocities it was committing on a daily basis almost defy belief. The more they did, the more popular the Mojahedin became for those who had no objection to their relationship with Iraq. The regime was in crisis and perhaps only the war kept it from being destroyed. The war allowed it to focus popular attention away from its domestic failures and its repression and the intense international pressure and condemnation. But this only worked up to a point.

The Mojahedin inside Iran, though diminished, carried out operation after operation and dealt telling blows to the regime's authorities. On the border, the NLA carried out its own military campaign and made some gains. In the West, the Mojahedin could count on massive support among the Iranian community who saw their successes. Demonstrations were organised in most major capitals and other major cities of the USA. Thousands attended. The Mojahedin were enjoying massive success. The demonstrations were backed by various organisations including unions, and financed by practically every political institution which would gain popularity by showing that they were against the regime. Delegations of the PMOI and the NCRI were permanently represented in the annual conferences of the International Socialist Organisation, the Labour Party (when in opposition) and the Trades Union Congress. They successfully lobbied the British and every European parliament, as well as the US Congress and House of Representatives. Most parliamentarians were more than happy to sign anything the Mojahedin presented if it showed their anti-Khomeini credentials to electors. Mojahedin statements carried priority in every news agency.

However, the Ideological Revolution carried with it its own imperatives which eventually impacted on the Mojahedin's 'diplomacy section' and their foreign policy in ways which though palpable to the outside world, were hard to quantify without understanding the internal relations which drove the changes.

In simple terms, Massoud Rajavi's agenda evolved from gaining power for himself as leader of the Mojahedin in Iran, to exerting his power over not only the Mojahedin members, but over the global community.

Since arriving in Paris in 1981, France had offered the Mojahedin as much help as was needed to establish the organisation as a significant threat to, and potential replacement for, Khomeini's administration. In response, France expected some conformity to the Western concept of an opposition force. Rajavi however, was unable to work to anyone else's agenda even when it was in his own favour.

France had been under increasing diplomatic pressure from Iran to stop the Mojahedin using Paris to co-ordinate attacks inside Iran and in 1986 France asked Rajavi to leave.

Rajavi, seeking never to expose himself to possible criticism from within the Mojahedin, did not admit to the members that he was being threatened with expulsion. Instead, he told his followers that since their victory was imminent, the next step for the Mojahedin, was to leave Europe and go right to the doorstep of Iran and to prepare for a military campaign that would win them back their country, and finally install the Mojahedin in power. He reasoned that there was only one possible place to go and that was Iraq, which was already providing all kinds of facilities including arms and land. He countered arguments against this plan.

They couldn't, for example, move to the United States of America simply because it was too far removed from Iran. This argument really shows Rajavi's propensity for action rather than dialogue. In fact politically, the Mojahedin could have gained enormously by moving to the USA. After all, America was the implacable enemy of the mullahs and, in spite of the Mojahedin's history of killing Americans while they were in Iran, was possibly willing to give them full backing had they shown themselves even a little compliant. But Rajavi wanted to be closer to what he perceived to be his real power base, that is the armed forces of the Mojahedin. Unable to break free from the belief that force was the only way forward, he had a vision, that was these forces carrying him and Maryam triumphantly atop a Chieftain tank, all the way to Tehran. Rajavi dismissed suggestions that the Mojahedin decamp to Pakistan or any other country. He wanted to be as physically close as possible to his goal. But in the age of supersonic travel, this argument simply does not add up.

Rajavi's real motive for going to Iraq was that he knew he could develop the close relation he had already built with Saddam Hussein. Saddam was willing, furthermore, to provide Rajavi with land and facilities with which to convert his armed struggle into military capacity. For the West, this was also a good solution. Rajavi's strategy of seven-sevenths had so far failed and he needed the help Iraq was willing to give. Saddam had also failed to gain in his war with Iran and his forces had been pushed back. The West was willing to help them both to work together and become more efficient.

Rajavi headquartered himself in Iraq and set about doing work for anyone and everyone in order to get money from anywhere he could. The Mojahedin became mercenaries for Saddam Hussein, providing intelligence gathered from inside Iran, which would help his war effort, buying equipment which Iraq couldn't do on her own behalf, etc.

A New Image

In 1987, the National Liberation Army was founded. Rajavi publicised this in glossy magazines distributed to all the political and media channels in the West. He needed to show that his army was a real threat to the regime. But he also wanted to show that it was different from any previous opposition army and certainly different from the Iraqi army. This army wouldn't degenerate into a mercenary or terrorist force. It had a woman in command. This grabbed attention in the West. The Mojahedin were riding high. But as ever, they were soon confronted with an unpalatable reality.

Primarily, the major question which Rajavi couldn't address was simply that as time passed, and year after year saw the Islamic Revolution becoming more and more established in Iran, particularly after the end of the war with Iraq and the death of Khomeini, was there any hope of a counter-revolution? How was it possible to survive as a 'revolutionary' organisation when the revolution had occurred for good or bad and they were excluded from any part in directing its future by being beyond the national borders? The West was willing to bet on the Mojahedin and its army as long as it saw hope in this. Rajavi, unable as ever to work to a wider agenda than his own, time and time again passed up proffered opportunities, and trashed the gains he had made through disastrous decisions. The worst of these was to go to Iraq with Western blessings, but to stay during the Gulf War when it was possible to have withdrawn. This meant that in the West, many found it impossible to continue with the same level of support.

On the surface, the Mojahedin were doing well in their external relations. They extracted support from all and sundry. Only the media were properly sceptical. Politicians and others readily signed pre-prepared statements condemning the human rights abuses and supporting the NCRI. The NCRI, after all, looked good. They had glossy magazines, and they held demonstrations in which thousands of exiled Iranians waved banners in their support. The NCRI claimed to represent every part of Iranian society, including Armenian Christians, Zoroastrians, Kurds, and more. That these members were co-opted from within the Mojahedin themselves was never exposed. The Mojahedin have always been excellent propagandists and have still managed to maintain the face of the NCRI as their political wing. But in spite of this success, Rajavi couldn't prevent himself from intervention.

In order to progress his Internal Revolution, Rajavi decided that he would promote women into all the leading roles. At the same time, he couldn't trust anyone inside the Mojahedin. He had to keep changing the personnel in every position. His system remains stable because he has sacrificed effectiveness for control. So he no longer has the well-respected, non-Mojahedin, Bahman Etemad acting as the NCRI spokesman in the UK. He first made Etemad answer to a 'sister' who most often had no English language let alone any knowledge of politics or diplomacy. Her job was simply to make sure that the NCRI spokesman only did what he was told.

After a while, Etemad was replaced by a Mojahedin 'sister' who speaks English and has been educated in the West, but who obeys Rajavi without question, rather than the needs of the political relationships. As such she is incapable of the social niceties and political subtleties which make up such relations. In the end, the underlying diplomatic and political relationships with politicians are sacrificed. It ends up with just lists of politicians who sign, and the basic understanding and support is gone. The Mojahedin of course were always willing to pay anyone who would offer them continued political support.

All their approaches eventually ring hollow. The issue of women for example, amounts to little more than having a women only layer at the top of the Mojahedin, between Rajavi and any other men. In their external relations they use it to say that they promote women's freedom, while at the same time, pointing to the regime's backward and suppressive treatment of women. On the surface this may look true. But no one in Rajavi's organisation is free, neither men nor women. So, their assertion is not as true as it seems.

The Gabon crisis

'Arrest of a number of sympathisers of the Mojahedin by French police. After Khomeini's terrorists released two French hostages, and the French government released Khomeini's terrorist diplomat, Vahid Gorgi, French police raided the residences of supporters of the Mojahedin and subsequently expelled fourteen of them to Gabon. A wave of outrage swept through France and other countries. After a month long international campaign for the return to France of the expelled refugees, an agreement was signed between a Mojahedin delegation and the Government of France, according to which all the expelled refugees returned to France.'

NLA Quarterly Autumn 1988

The failure of the years outside Iran and its shrinking support and forces had its impact on the Western appraisal of the Mojahedin. In 1986, France had asked the Mojahedin not to use Paris, and over 200 telephone lines, as their base for carrying out attacks on Iran. For Rajavi it became obvious that he had to show some results or the situation would deteriorate for him. The only way was to accept the exposure of his relationship with Saddam Hussein and Iraq. He had to pay the political price for the money and bases he had gained there. France was only too happy to get rid of them and avoid being accused of harbouring terrorists in France, which the Iranians had raised with the United Nations. At that time, Iraq also had good relations with France and could be relied upon not to use the Mojahedin card against Iran without consultation, (at least France thought this was the case).

The Gabon crisis arose due to the unwillingness of the Mojahedin to totally cut ties with France. After asking them to leave several times, in December 1987 France took action to close their bases completely. In order to put pressure on the Mojahedin, fourteen of their members were expelled and sent to a prison in Gabon, a former French colony in Africa.

The Mojahedin response was to threaten to uncover all the details of their relations with France and hunger strikes were started in front of French embassies across Europe. Mehdi Abrishamchi was dispatched to Paris where he threatened the French Foreign Minister that they would burn themselves in front of the office (they had already gone on hunger strike) and reveal everything.

Francois Mitterand's envoy to Iran later explained that he had achieved agreement with Rafiqdoust in Tehran; that Iran free the captured French nationals along with some other deals, and in return, France would free some Iranian terrorists, excluding Anis Naghash. Some other Iranian demands were not accepted. However, at 4 a.m. he received a telephone call saying that there were problems and the deal was off and that he had better come straight to Rafiqdoust's office.

The following day when he was travelling to the airport, the driver told him 'it was your own fault, you did not give as much as the others would give'. The envoy later discovered that while he was negotiating, there was another delegation from Paris representing Jacques Chirac. They had agreed to give Anis Naghash and to expel the Mojahedin. Of course the referendum was near. Later, when the time came to release Naghash, Mitterand as President, refused to sign the paper and started playing up. The same posturing occurred over the Mojahedin, but they took it personally and escalated the issue. France was unwilling to get involved in a bigger crisis, and knowing that the Mojahedin could be easily controlled (by now they had enough people inside the Mojahedin working for them) with the agreement of the Iranian regime, France backed off and returned the deportees. But the telephone lines were withheld and their activities were curtailed.

In some ways, the Gabon crisis was useful to Rajavi as yet another crisis, which he turned to his benefit. He was able to present it to the Iranian community outside Iran as yet another attack by the Iranian regime against the legitimate resistance movement. So that when he wanted to round people up and press-gang them into going to Iraq for Forouq only a few months later, he had a ready audience. That is, many ordinary Iranians who had developed an interest and sympathy over the

Gabon episode were persuaded into leaping to their defence and victory in Iraq.

The Mojahedin's role in the Gulf War and afterwards

In March 1991, after the defeat of Iraq at the hands of the allied forces, Rajavi's troops helped Saddam Hussein contain the Kurdish rebellions in the north. The NLA troops were ordered to raze Kurdish villages and fire on civilian populations there. The Morvarid (Pearl) operation took place in March 1991 when NLA tanks moved in to repress a Kurdish uprising. This was feted as a huge success. For the first time, women only tank crews went into battle. What an achievement! But the success of women tank crews did not divert attention away from the NLA's role in suppressing Kurds. Human Rights Watch later gave out a report on this issue condemning the role of the Mojahedin. Many members had refused to carry out these orders and were later subjected to 'court martial', ending up in prisons and then Iraqi refugee camps and forced to endure years of suffering.

This use of the Mojahedin is not surprising. Rajavi has been using the resources of Saddam only for them to be deployed on a rainy day like this. The former Director of Saddam's Military Intelligence, General Vafigh Samerai, who defected from Iraq and now lives in London, revealed a great deal about Saddam's Intelligence activities. Including the relationship with the Mojahedin, and other groups which are paid for their services. He revealed who was responsible for them, who their contacts were to issue orders from the Intelligence Ministry, what was expected of them and how Rajavi would be paid for each of these services, including intelligence gathering and special assignments.

After the Gulf War, the Mojahedin's star was waning. Though not treated as pariahs in political and media circles, they were certainly looked upon with greater suspicion and distrust. Rajavi, desperate to make up ground, began to field the defunct NCRI again as a democratic alternative. He began to make use of the women's issue in public. He sent Maryam to Europe to court political good will. But none of this had any real success.

The West had begun to make its rapprochement with Iran, and after Seyed Mohammad Khatami was elected in 1997, the country looked to have very different prospects to those the Mojahedin was advertising.

One of the choices that hurt the Mojahedin most was their deliberate and close relationship with Saddam Hussein. This has always been a controversial move, and one for which Rajavi has paid a high price. Before anything else, Rajavi could not and still cannot, give up the benefits he enjoys from being in Iraq. He could possibly have moved his organisation elsewhere and especially during the Gulf War in 1991. This was his golden political opportunity to make rapprochement with the West and wash his hands of Saddam, make a new start and, backed by the West, become a serious contender for the future government of Iran. But he couldn't let go of his benefits. Rajavi can't share anything and he can't work to someone else's agenda, even if that coincides with his own. Which is in strange contrast to his mercenary tendencies when it comes to doing all sorts of dirty work for money. In fact he cannot pay the price for later gain, that is, to risk paying from his own pocket.

He would not give up Saddam because this was 'cash' and everything else had a condition attached. He tried to keep what he already had and gain more as well. But it doesn't work like that. Now he is thinking of returning to the West because he can see that everything he has is being lost to him, especially now that Iran and Iraq are developing their relations and he is getting less help from Saddam. He can only therefore, survive by creating crises. So, terrorism inside Iran and a restructuring of the organisation itself presented themselves as Rajavi's only way forward.

If Rajavi had done what he was supposed to do when he left Iran, none of this would have come about. The NCRI, had it grown and worked with other opposition groups, had a good future and was backed by the West, desperate to find a way to get rid of Khomeini. But Rajavi didn't want to be a representative or a member of a coalition, he wanted to be the sole leader, and he couldn't wait until the NCRI was installed as the interim government in Iran.

Chapter 11

RAJAVI'S SECOND BID FOR POWER

Operation Forouq-e Javidan

The West was on the whole, extremely supportive of the Mojahedin's struggle. But this all went wrong in 1988. This was the defeat which was never admitted to, and Rajavi tried to carry on afterwards as though nothing had happened. But although he could use his propaganda machine to convince his own supporters who had no access to the media in the Iraqi camps, the Western political scene was a different matter. They quickly assessed the failure of Forouq in their own plans, and the failure of Saddam Hussein to prevail in the war and defeat Khomeini.

Of course, Saddam knew that better than anyone else. Very soon after he accepted the ceasefire and soon after giving up his ambition to defeat the Persians, he settled for less, that is the invasion of Kuwait. Accepting the ceasefire with Iran prompted those countries which had given him money and arms, to reclaim the debt. It was deeply humiliating for Saddam, who regarded himself as leader of all the Arabs fighting the Persians and Israel, to have a small insignificant country like Kuwait ask for its money back!

In line with the strategy of destabilising the Iranian regime, in June 1988, the NLA undertook a military operation, Chelcheraq or 'Forty Stars', which, with the backing of Iraqi forces, penetrated deeper than ever into Iranian territory. Rajavi was determined to use the NLA to push a path for himself and

Maryam into Tehran. In this operation, they reached Mehran, a small sized town in the direction of Hammedan. The Mojahedin managed to capture Mehran with the help of some of the townsfolk, who, with typical pragmatism, welcomed the invading force. The Mojahedin held Mehran for a few days, before retreating with a handful of new members who had decided to join them. So much for their popular support, only around fifteen young people joined them despite their clear success in this operation. After all, they were going back to Iraq in wartime.

The Mojahedin have only ever undertaken military operations into Iran with full liaison with the Iraqi military, commanded by Saddam Hussein. The Iraqi military provided training and logistical support, and maps from reconnaissance flights over the proposed route. The Iraqis agreed to bomb Iranian positions twenty-four hours before the start of any Mojahedin operation in order to put the Iranian forces on the defensive and to create disarray. Only with all this support would the Mojahedin start their offensive. In the case of Chelcheraq, the Mojahedin agreed with the Iraqis that they would advance and the Iraqis would follow on behind to capture any spoils of war, such as artillery. Instead, however, the Iraqis built trenches and dug-in on the captured territory, making military gains on the back of the Mojahedin's idealism.

But then without warning, in July 1988, the eight-year war between Iran and Iraq came to an end when Saddam Hussein gave up on his strategy and sued for peace. Khomeini reluctantly accepted to end the war and accept Iran's victory. By this time Iraq had not only been pushed back from all the Iranian territory which it had invaded, but had suffered major defeats on his own territory in Fab and Basra. In spite of this, Khomeini likened accepting the peace agreement to drinking from the 'poisoned chalice', even on Iran's terms as victor. So useful was the war to his regime in maintaining its hold on power.

As far as the Mojahedin were concerned, they had also analysed the benefits of war to Khomeini and firmly bet on its continuation. This sudden cessation of hostilities now heralded what might be the last chance they had to launch an all out attack across the border into Iran. With the two countries at peace and the borders under dispute or at least under intense scrutiny, it would be impossible for the foreseeable future to cross with an army, especially because they would have to rely on Iraqi air force support which was essential to any such incursion. Rajavi ordered his organisation to ready themselves in two weeks for their triumphant march on Tehran. He assessed that the country was ready. After years of war and repression, surely the people would welcome the Mojahedin as the liberating force it purported to be. However, the real reason that Rajavi acted so quickly, was simply that he could not leave it any longer.

He asked Saddam Hussein for support, which was unwillingly granted. It was clear to the Iraqi military, that Rajavi's plan was an impossible task. They agreed to give air and missile support up to a certain range. This was performed. The Iraqi Air Force flew overhead and long range missiles were used.

Once the ground attack commenced the Mojahedin traversed just as far as this support went and not a metre beyond it. 150 kilometres into Iranian territory, they passed a gorge and crossed a large plain before entering a second gorge, Chahar Zabar. The Iranian army, which had intelligence of their plans, arranged a simple ambush, surrounding them between the two gorges. They stopped the Mojahedin in their tracks, killing over 2,000 of them. Those who were bringing up the rear immediately retreated back to Iraq. Of those who were caught in the trap, some managed to escape and went forward into Iran, some eventually making their way out via Pakistan. Some moved off toward Kurdistan, and made their way back from there. Others simply wandered lost and hungry for several days before being able to get help from local villagers or tribes people. The operation was a debacle.

On several levels the operation was a disaster in the making. Firstly, because Rajavi sent many completely untrained and unarmed 'troops' into the battle. These were young Iranian men and women who were living in the West. Some had been recruited as recently as during the Gabon hunger strike just a few months earlier. As many supporters as could be persuaded were hurriedly sent to Iraq, given a few days basic training and then expected to go on a military operation to invade Iran; something the Iraqis had failed to do after eight years. These people were sent as if on a picnic with watermelons, bread and milk and other unlikely foodstuffs to keep them going until they arrived in Tehran.

The people who were sent included old men and women (parents and grandparents of the combatants) and youths under eighteen years of age. Children, old women and foreigners were sent with their passports and documents in their pockets, to confront battle hardened, experienced commandos from Iran, with air force backing. One foreign national, a French nurse and wife of a Mojahedin supporter, was captured by the Iranians and eventually returned to France. Others were not so fortunate. Among those killed were Sue and Samina from Britain.

Even many of the members of the Mojahedin who had been through some military training were individuals totally unsuited to a military campaign. Members of the Mojahedin's 'diplomacy' section, who were Western educated, middle class Iranians, simply hadn't the temperament for fighting. The Iranian army, which they faced, had fought Iraq for eight long years. They were battle hardened. Some were uncouth villagers who had no compunction in killing an enemy with their bare hands, Iraqi or Iranian. Others were ideologically geared up to target and kill the Mojahedin as the enemy of their revered Imam's revolution. From the outset it was a grossly uneven match.

If the operation hadn't been ambushed it is still hard to see how it would have succeeded in capturing city after city and garnering support all the way to Tehran with such a hotchpotch army. However, perhaps this is too harsh a criticism and an underestimation of the readiness of the people of Iran for a change of government. Perhaps, if the Mojahedin had been able to progress further into Iranian territory, events could have gained momentum and the counter-revolution started. This, surely was the only possible time for that to happen.

113

As it happened, Iran's army ridiculously easily ambushed the operation. It was a massacre, with two thousand people killed because there was nowhere for them to escape.

Examples of incompetence in Forouq

The Iraqi military believed that the plan was foolhardy and almost certain to fail. Their assessment was based on military considerations. However, the Mojahedin had their own internal weaknesses, which also played a large part in the failure of the operation. The most damaging aspect was the command structure of the army. Since the Ideological Revolution, only those who accepted Rajavi's leadership and passed the ideological tests were deemed capable of leadership. This was because they were loyal to Rajavi and would obey his every command. However, in a military operation it meant that those who led most often had no real military training and experience.

An example of the damaging effect of this, was the misuse of troops and equipment. The Mojahedin brought with them a big artillery gun from Kerend (the city which in theory they had captured) and took it to Chahar Zebar to use to fight their way through. They lost many people getting it through the regime's ambushes only to find that the gun was too big to use and that it would only have been useful if it had been left in Kerend. One of the Mojahedin who had previously been a soldier in Iran's army, had told them this, but as the Mojahedin command structure demanded, no one was prepared to listen to an ordinary soldier.

Many survivors later said that when they were confronted with the enemy, they hesitated to shoot. This is a normal civilian mentality and therefore many like them got killed. Others, out of ignorance, took cover under vehicles when they saw enemy aircraft approach and then burned to death when the planes targeted the vehicles. Many were shocked and demoralised when they saw what had been done to the captured Mojahedin, especially the women. Only between ten and twenty percent of the Mojahedin engaged in Chahar Zabar returned to their bases in Iraq defeated and depleted. Many were injured, many very seriously.

When it was over, the Iraqis merely said 'I told you so'. During the whole operation, Rajavi was flying back and forth between Baghdad, and the Iraqi Centre of Command, begging Saddam to engage more of his air force and break the ambush either for a forward advance or a retreat. Saddam and his military knew there was no point in risking more Iraqi lives and planes to rescue the Mojahedin forces and therefore refused his requests. It was too late and they had warned Rajavi in advance how much air support they were willing to give.

Rajavi's reaction

But Rajavi would not show that he thought it had been a failure or a mistake. His publicity machine went into overdrive about how afraid the regime had been of this attack. How it had shaken the regime to its roots. In fact, it was a surprise for the regime in Iran; they could not accept it or believe it, but not in the way that Rajavi depicted. During the ambush operation and for some time afterwards, they were still waiting for the real attack, for something major to happen. They couldn't believe that this incompetent incursion was all the Mojahedin had to offer and that nothing else happened. They were expecting an attack by Iraq in some other part of the country, or for some other foreign power to attack, or even for an internal coup d'état to be staged. But nothing further happened.

Seeing that he couldn't challenge the truth, Rajavi later changed the goal posts and began to use ideological arguments to explain the operation, carefully avoiding any hint that he regarded it as a failure. Using Maryam as his mouthpiece, he claimed that the Mojahedin were not pure enough and didn't deserve a victory. The leader, Maryam said, had done the maximum he could, but his followers, except Maryam of course, had betrayed him because their minds were immersed in other things, such as their spouse, their children and their families. Rajavi began his usual round of meetings to manipulate the members' perception. Starting from the top people, he had everyone confess that they had betrayed him, going as far as to say that they didn't actually want to be victorious.

More reactions to Forouq

Inside Iran, the reaction was severe. In fact the regime had been shaken by the surprise attack and its response was to kill many of the political prisoners who were languishing in the country's jails, just for good measure. So Rajavi was responsible not only for the deaths of the 2,000 who were directly involved in Forouq, but also for the deaths of tens of hundreds of political prisoners who might otherwise have been released after a few years. Rajavi characteristically claimed that all these people had died for him, in order for him to come to power in Iran. This, by any calculation, is untrue. These individuals were killed because they believed that they were fighting for the freedom of their country and their people from the despotic rule of Khomeini. The trust they had in their leader was that he was struggling for the same ends.

Rajavi had his own agenda. He claimed that those killed in Forouq-e Javidan, were not sufficiently devoted to him and were fighting for their own goals and aims, for nationalistic or personal motives, out of love or hate or whatever. Therefore, in his mind, those who died had not passed the phase of Ideological Revolution in order to be considered as fighting for him. This is blatant hypocrisy. On one hand Rajavi claims that the political prisoners who were executed in Iran died for him, but on the other hand, he accuses his members in Iraq of not being considered as having fought for him.

It is surely true to say that the Mojahedin as a cult is presently in a position to claim that its remaining members really do believe in this so-called ideology and are fighting simply for love of Rajavi. Also that they do not accept any personal or social responsibility for what they are doing. These people are capable of performing suicide bombing or any other task they could be called upon by the leader. However, Rajavi isn't interested in the freedom of people, he only wants power. If Iran had a freely elected democratic and secular government, Rajavi would still go on fighting. The devoted members have long said that and as a religious cult they see democracy as a means, not an end in itself. Only if something is useful for their purposes will they pursue it, particularly for their foreign

116

relations with the West. Rajavi wants to be the only leader of Iran, or anywhere. So he claims that these people have died for him in order to gain credit.

Forouq-e Javidan is another example of Rajavi misusing the resources of the organisation for his own benefit. In this case again, the resources were its people. Of course, if people accept the concept of an ideological leader, that is, if they reject democracy, then it is Rajavi's right to use every resource for his goal. In his own analysis, Rajavi applies his own version of the evolution of animals to the political scene. For him it is as simple as sacrificing a chicken or a sheep for the more evolved species, human beings. What he means is that it is okay for those lower down the ideological chain to be sacrificed for those higher up. Rajavi says

> 'the rules of leadership differ from the rules for followers'.

After Forouq, Rajavi stated that 'the blood of those martyred has insured the future of the Mojahedin'. This means that so many new killings are insurance against Iran moving towards liberalism or democracy for some time. It was also true after 30th Khordad and on other occasions, that by radicalising the atmosphere, both the Mojahedin and the hardliners in Iran have gained, and the democratic and liberal forces have suffered most. No room will be left for them and their ideas, as people cry for blood and vengeance. The problem is that this path has to be kept hot and once they have started, they have to continue and shed more blood in order to keep the atmosphere hot.

Forouq signalled another wave of dissenters who left the organisation shortly afterwards. Nothing could be done to prevent this. The organisation was at its lowest ebb since 1972 when all of the leaders were executed.

Longer term effects

Even though it had always been assumed that the death of Khomeini would be a positive turning point in the Mojahedin's strategy for gaining power, when Ayatollah Khomeini eventually died on 3rd June 1989, the Mojahedin were badly placed to react. They were massively depleted in terms of members, resources and morale. For Rajavi, it looked as though the way was blocked for him to get to Tehran. Yet another bid for power had failed, and no explanation was given. But the West were still prepared to bank on the Mojahedin – there was no one else and at least they had proved themselves willing to try whatever their motives.

Rajavi was faced with a dilemma after the failure of Forouq. Even his most ardent of supporters could barely pretend to themselves after this, that there would be a revolution in Iran and that the Mojahedin would be able to lead it. Events simply moved too fast for this to be a real possibility. Although Khomeini hated the idea of peace because he feared it would expose the internal repression, in fact the peace brought with it a sense of stability, which did more than anything else to rob the Resistance of its impetus. But, faced with this lack of impetus, and the changes on the political scene once Khomeini had died, what was Rajavi to do? He wasn't inside the country to take part in the political process no matter how unlikely this might have been in reality.

It was still keenly felt by political observers, that the Mojahedin as a political force, was being sidelined by the power struggle taking place inside the country. In some way, Rajavi had to change the nature of the Mojahedin in order to challenge the changing scene inside Iran. On the other hand, faced with peace and stability, he had to ensure that the regime did not settle its debts and begin to make progress. The only way he could stop progress inside Iran was to start a terrorist campaign. He probably hoped that this would be the same as the guerrilla warfare, which ensued after 20th June 1981. But following the abortive military campaigns of the NLA, and the growing stability of the regime, this kind of local armed resistance activity could only take the shape of terrorist activities.

This became more obvious after the failure of Maryam to make or remake any ties with the West, when Rajavi deployed her in Europe in 1993 as 'President elect for the future Iran'. Rajavi, seeing the failure of the NLA on the horizon, tried to go back to the past and the old strategy of killing ordinary officials, placing bombs here and there. A policy he had described in Paris before the formation of the NLA as 'cutting the fingertips of the regime'. But this was a strategy, which had already failed and he had moved to Iraq to create the NLA in response.

This latest attempt at armed struggle failed and is failing for obvious reasons. The most obvious reason is because the average age of the Mojahedin's members is forty years and over. These members who left Iran in the early 1980s or before, cannot even remember the streets of their cities or towns. They cannot survive in a hostile environment for even a few hours. Even though they declare willing, they do not really expect Rajavi to send them inside Iran after twenty years, and they are not really willing to go. So Rajavi must rely on people who have been newly recruited, such as one young man who had done his military service in Iran before escaping as a refugee in 1996. When the Mojahedin recruited him and took him to Iraq after only a few months, he was almost immediately sent into Iran on a terrorist mission because of his up to date knowledge of the city where he had served as a soldier.

From the other side, the regime was now established and would not allow them to build on these attacks. Also, more importantly, the help from ordinary people which they could count on before, had, since the Ideological Revolution and Rajavi's move to Iraq, diminished to practically nothing.

Another problem for the Mojahedin has been infiltration. The military attempts are failing due to the desperation of their recruitment policy, which has led to heavy infiltration of their ranks. The organisation is now so thoroughly infiltrated, that out of four recent terrorist attempts, three teams were immediately arrested at the border and the other one before they were able to undertake any action, because of intelligence that reached the regime via these infiltrators.

The Mojahedin claimed the assassination of Sarhang Shirazi, a retired general, but later, the killers were discovered to be from a hard line group within the regime. It is still not clear whether the Mojahedin were in co-operation with this group or whether they were simply being opportunist in claiming responsibility. One mortar was launched into a teachers' residence in Tehran instead of the supposed military target. One bomb was left in a rubbish bin outside the High Court in Tehran injuring passers by. Another mortar landed in a public park, injuring a young woman.

From a political point of view, time has changed and the Mojahedin no longer have the international support or legitimacy for carrying out these acts against Iran from Iraq.

Chapter 12

INTERNAL RELATIONS

With the brutal failure of his second bid for power with the Forouq-e Javidan operation in 1988, and the rapid political changes to Iran after Khomeini's death, Rajavi knew he must speedily change the identity of the Mojahedin to confront the new challenges. More than anything, he needed to keep his own members loyal while at the same time, continue to present a viable and desirable alternative for Western consumption. One of the ways he achieved this was to give up the pretence that the NCRI was somehow a separate body and convert it into the political wing of the Mojahedin, or as he described the new order, the Iranian Resistance. But beyond this cosmetic change he needed a different approach to the dynamics of the Iranian political scene.

Now that the motivation of 'Khomeini' had gone, Rajavi had to find a new way to inspire his followers to obey him. So he began to change his own previous version of things. He now described the organisation's ideology as global, rather than just being for Iran. The Mojahedin's mission was now to take the Ideological Revolution and its message for women to the whole world not just to Iran. The Mojahedin's ideology was transformed from simply being a tool for Rajavi to recharge his followers' zeal in their fight with Khomeini, into an end in itself.

Immediately after Forouq-e Javidan and the death of Khomeini, Rajavi faced a dual crisis. In Iran, the leadership contest was taking place. Who would or could replace Khomeini was the critical issue for the world, not just for Iranians. Ayatollah Montazeri was still under house arrest in Qom for his outspoken criticisms of Khomeini's treatment of opposition groups. The next natural successor in terms of religious qualification had been an Ayatollah several years older than Khomeini who had died just before Khomeini had. In the end, Ayatollah Ali Khamenei was chosen, not because of his religious credentials – he had to be 'promoted' in order to undertake the role – but because he was committed to preserving the ruling system that Khomeini had built over the previous nine years.

In 1981, the Mojahedin, knowing they couldn't last long in Iran, burned all its remaining resources in Iran in an attempt to force the issue and provoke a counter-revolution. They wanted to remove anyone who could possibly be a successor to Khomeini after he died. They blew up the Jomhouri Eslami Party headquarters killing over seventy top people from the regime. They succeeded in killing Ayatollah Beheshti, who would most likely have succeeded Khomeini. Beheshti was the top strategic player for the regime and had good international ties. He was both political and diplomatic. This represented a serious blow to the regime. They also assassinated Ayatollah Dast Gheib in a suicide bombing and attempted to kill Khamenei but failed, although he lost the use of one hand as a result of the attack.

Now Ayatollah Khamenei wasn't about to let go all the gains made by the 'reactionaries'. But Rajavi regarded it as a personal insult to be pitched against someone whom he regarded as his inferior. He couldn't let go of Khomeini, and was lost for some time after his personal enemy had gone. His 'raison d'être' as he called it was no more. It rankled to have his enemy demoted to what he regarded was the level of a second rate ayatollah. Rajavi continued to refer to 'the Khomeini regime' long after it could no longer be described as such.

Inside the Mojahedin after Forouq-e Javidan, Rajavi was faced with a different kind of crisis, a crisis of confidence. If he allowed any doubt at all to creep in over his leadership then the organisation, or at least his version of it, was doomed. He started with his manipulation of members' perception of the events and turned it into an ideological matter in which he had been betrayed by the members' lack of faith in him.

After Forouq-e Javidan there were many forced marriages. Those who had lost a spouse during the operation, were 'compensated' by having another spouse provided by the munificence of the leader, Rajavi. Many objected in their souls, but such is the peer pressure and the need to conform and so lowly is the person who has not passed each ideological phase as it arises, that nearly everyone submitted to the doling out of partners.

For women it was both a duty and a reward. Under Maryam's tutelage they were supposed to regard men as holding them back, blocking their freedom. Men were exploiters of women. The women were awarded a husband on the unspoken understanding that because all their love was for the leaders, they would have no need for a husband and would very quickly 'reject' him in favour of devotion to Sister Maryam. The bitter resentment felt by these women at being 'given' away to a man to replace his dead wife, worked supremely in Rajavi's favour. He couldn't have hoped for a better opportunity to create the necessary tensions between the sexes that his next phase required.

In this atmosphere of doubt and change, Rajavi's next step was bold. Drawing on the 1985 rewrite of Mojahedin ideology, he now divorced the Mojahedin totally from its original structure and ethos.

In October 1989, Rajavi announced the next phase in his Ideological Revolution, the 'Internal Revolution'. It became known as such because this phase, unlike the marriage, was not made public. In fact the Mojahedin did all they could to keep this development hidden from outsiders. However, in essence it was simply another step toward Rajavi's original goal, the total control over all Mojahedin members, which he started in 1985.

The content of the Internal Revolution was simple enough on the surface. Maryam was introduced as Secretary General of the People's Mojahedin Organisation of Iran. Until now, Massoud and Maryam had jointly led the Mojahedin. Now Maryam was solely in charge. The announcement caused a huge shock throughout the membership. The unspoken dread, which struck the hearts of loyal members, was simply this – what then, has happened to our beloved Massoud?

The fear was manipulated deliberately because Rajavi was now about to announce himself as the supreme ideological leader of the whole Iranian Resistance movement. This placed him above not only the Mojahedin organisation, but also above the National Liberation Army (which in theory had many non-Mojahedin and therefore non-ideological members fighting in its ranks) and above the NCRI of which the Mojahedin was in theory at this stage only one member out of eleven. In one fell swoop, Rajavi had 'promoted' himself above Maryam to 'Leader of the Resistance' which in effect meant nothing but total ideological leader of everyone and everything; the one person who decides everything for everyone. The full implication of this took some time to emerge. For the present, everyone was relieved that he was still 'in charge'. Deep down, every member knew that Maryam couldn't replace Rajavi as the real leader, and this is what Rajavi himself had made them believe.

The method by which Rajavi introduced this new phase was as significant as the actual changes. It exposed Rajavi's use of the techniques typically used in all cults to manipulate the thought processes of the membership. In Iraq, Rajavi arranged a meeting of unprecedented importance for all Mojahedin members. Members were flown in from around the world to attend. All but the most essential activities were stopped. The meeting took five days to complete. Rajavi spoke from late in the evening when everyone had completed their daily duties, until the early hours of the morning, when the members were allowed a little sleep before again going about their daily tasks. In the hot, stuffy atmosphere of the huge auditorium in Ashraf camp, the members sat and listened to Rajavi expounding on his philosophy.

His oratorical technique was one well known in Persian philosophy. But where the true philosophers use allegory and allusion in order to illuminate a difficult concept, Rajavi used them to more deeply confound his audience. His aim was to introduce religious stories familiar to Shiite Muslims, and give a modern personal interpretation which linked into the politics of armed struggle and opposition. The ready audience was swept along on emotional waves without understanding the real import behind the allusions and stories. Rajavi's intention was to charge them with religious and revolutionary fervour and then, as usual in these meetings, have a few pre-tutored individuals 'interpret' his message to the members. His message 'I am the next Imam, I am your link with God' was implied rather than actually said.

Previous to the five-day neshast, Rajavi had summoned Fahimeh Arvani, who worked closely with Maryam, and charged her up with his new ideas. He then read her subsequent reports to a selected few, thereby charging them so that in the big neshast, everybody had to agree that she knew things that they did not. That is, Fahimeh was totally devoted to Maryam because this was the only way to understand even a little of Rajavi's greatness. Only Maryam had been able so far to perceive Rajavi's true greatness.

In this five-day neshast, apparently only Fahimeh Arvani fully understood the Mojahedin's ideology. She stood up on cue to tearfully declare her love for the leaders. Of course, love for Rajavi was taken for granted, what was actually required was that every individual member love Maryam as the only funnel for their love for Rajavi. Maryam was now placed below Rajavi in the hierarchy and all the members were invited to love her. It was said that no one but Maryam, could fully appreciate Rajavi and therefore only she could act as the channel for every members' love and devotion for him and because he was the embodiment of their struggle, that meant for the benefit of the struggle. This placed Rajavi beyond understanding, beyond criticism, and beyond accountability.

In the end, the mistake that was made in choosing Fahimeh was that she wasn't the usual uneducated village woman that Rajavi usually chooses. Fahimeh had lived and studied in Germany for some time and she eventually came to see things that couldn't fool her for long. Maryam took her to Europe with her in 1993, leaving Shahrzad, her personal assistant, to work for Rajavi.

But it wasn't long before Maryam had to send Fahimeh back to Iraq. It was too dangerous for them to let her loose outside Iraq because she could no longer play the role expected of her. In effect, she had seen the nakedness of the emperor! The dilemma facing Rajavi then was that Fahimeh had been introduced to the organisation as one of its leaders. That is, one of the ideological leaders who, after Rajavi and Maryam, are the ones for whom the rules are different to those for ordinary members, one of those who should be given one hundred per cent obedience. This was to the extent that if anyone thinks they see any mistake in one of these leaders, they should look inside themselves to find out what is wrong with themselves. As Rajavi puts it, they are mirrors. Therefore, it was impossible to downgrade and demote her. She had to be kept under control and save her face, while allowing her no responsibility or any direct or serious contact with others.

Application of the Internal Revolution

The real purpose of this phase was to guarantee that there would be no leadership challenge. Rajavi had now removed himself from the ordinary level of leader and elevated himself beyond the normal leader's role to that of link with God. An unassailable position. Now, any leadership challenge could only be aimed at Maryam, and Rajavi ensured that this would not happen by an ingenious ploy of 'freeing women'. This irrevocably diverted the attention of the members from the question of leadership (this became unquestionable) to the difficulty that existed between men and women and their respective roles in the struggle.

Maryam was held up as an example to the women in the organisation. It was claimed that women could free themselves from their oppression as women, only by following her example. But although the move was a pretext for freeing the energy of the women in the organisation, it had the very real value of being able to exploit the women members' devotion, and keeping the men in a state of permanent confusion over their role.

In this equation the only weakness would be Maryam herself. There remained a possibility that she would start playing things her own way or trying to get more power or not delivering what was required from her. This was taken care of by marrying her and also by Rajavi having her completely under his thumb. Even so, he was aware of this minimum risk and many times said to her that 'either you will send me to the sky or will reduce me to nothing'. When she went to Europe, this disaster was imminent. Rajavi felt it and quickly took her back to Baghdad.

Logic?

The Internal Revolution proved much more difficult to impose than the Ideological Revolution. The Ideological Revolution required people to see the leadership differently. Most ordinary members were happy to do this because they revered Rajavi and believed he could do no wrong. Only the more politically astute or the real revolutionaries found anything to object to in this. However, with the Internal Revolution came the requirement to make painful changes for each member.

Soon after the five-day neshast, once the new leadership roles had been accepted, it was announced that every member should ideologically divorce from their spouse in order to devote one hundred percent of their love and energy to Rajavi.

For those who weren't married or who had lost a spouse in the military campaigns, this probably looked on the surface as something which, although it didn't really affect them directly, would in a sense, even things out. In other words, no member was married and there was no differentiation in their status or supposed privileges. But Rajavi didn't intend to leave anyone out, and the changes were soon discovered to be intended for everyone and to be far deeper in their personal impact than anyone could have imagined.

In the beginning, some married couples decided to leave. In other cases, one half of the partnership wanted to leave and take the children away. It was a time of upheaval. In the ensuing months and years, as the changes filtered down to the supporters, more and more people became disillusioned and began to leave. For many, the Mojahedin had clearly lost their way, and in the end, the difference of whether a member stayed or not became an issue of cult identity.

What Rajavi was asking everyone in the Mojahedin to do was to give him total obedience. He implied to them (through the mouths of Maryam and Fahimeh) that he had links with God and therefore knew things that ordinary members couldn't be expected to understand. This meant that anyone who rejected him was blaspheming against God. The members were mostly willing to allow themselves to be indoctrinated with this new concept.

For many, they had simply come too far to break away and to give up the struggle. Rajavi had been so proficient in destroying the strength and credibility of all the other groups and organisations which opposed Khomeini, that there really was no where else to go to continue the struggle. The longer members had served in the organisation and in particular the higher rank they had, the less likely they were to think critically, or even to think at all.

Rajavi was revered. It was a position he had carefully crafted for himself with his own propaganda. Like most 'dictators' he had been scrupulous about promoting a saintly yet authoritative image of himself for his followers. Rajavi's use of cult techniques had by this time, become so endemic in the organisation, that it began to function as a cult rather than a political or military organisation. During this period in particular, as members struggled to understand the new terms and conditions of membership, (with no manifesto to guide them) the struggle for power in Iran was all but forgotten and the struggle to keep up their membership and the privileges of rank gained in the ascendancy. Although everyone spoke of love, love for Massoud, love for Maryam, for many members the only feeling which this move engendered, was fear. They feared being found out or left behind. And the answer from above to everyone's questions was always the same; work harder, don't think, just follow Maryam's example.

As ever, Rajavi was 'saved' by external events. The Gulf War in 1991 provided a much needed distraction from the internal issues. He could now put to the test his members' resolve and their willingness to sacrifice for him. He didn't need to refer back to Forouq-e Javidan. Members were still smarting over his accusations of betrayal. They showed themselves more than willing this time to obey and sacrifice. Although none were killed (the allied forces deliberately avoided their bases) they unfortunately became implicated in the killing of Kurdish villagers on behalf of Saddam Hussein directly after the conflict ended.

More cynically still, Rajavi used the Gulf War as a pretext to have all the children removed from the bases in Iraq. The children had acted as a brake on the application of the Internal Revolution. Whilst the children were around, it provided an excuse for spouses to meet up in a family context. There was the possibility for 'divorced' couples to continue a covert relationship. Rajavi wanted the total devotion of everyone with no rivals. For him, the children represented his most dangerous rivals for their parents' affections and loyalties. So on the pretext of having them evacuated to safety during the allied bombing, he had children even as young as two months old, sent abroad where they were adopted by Iranian families or kept in dormitories.

Some of the older children soon returned to Iraq and though still under age, became members of the NLA. They were expected to 'reject' their parents as part of the new ideology. In other cases, a parent bravely refused to be separated and decided to accompany their children abroad. As usual, although the Mojahedin denounced these people as defectors, as weak and useless people, they did all they could to keep hold of them and have them work in their bases in the West. In all, the losses were few and Rajavi consolidated his hold over the members' minds, hearts and lives.

Reasons to stay

Given these difficult requirements imposed upon them by Rajavi, it is a serious question in the minds of many, as to why and how the members stay in the organisation. There are several reasons given, but in the end it adds up to the fact that the Mojahedin as a cult organisation has for years employed highly sophisticated mind control techniques. This means that even when a member believes they are thinking for his or herself, they in reality, have the context of their thoughts so limited and reduced, that only a few easily resolvable doubts surface into their conscious minds.

From the time of the Ideological Revolution there remain the same 'reasons to stay' churning around the heads of doubting members. For some there is simple self-delusion. After twenty years of struggle, they cannot accept that the organisation, for which they have sacrificed everything, has betrayed them. For others it is a matter of self-preservation. They have nowhere else to go. Certainly they feel safer there than anywhere else. Some, who joined directly from Iran, cannot imagine what it must be like in the West. The organisation deliberately paints an evil picture of what has become of those who have left. It is claimed they have become drug addicts and prostitutes, or they have been recruited by the Iranian regime and made to work against their erstwhile colleagues. This last claim has nearly reached saturation point. When the number of those accused of working for the Iranian regime is added up, it amounts to one recruit every twenty days over the past twenty years, an enviable record for any Intelligence Service.

There are some that still hope to ultimately gain a position and some degree of power by hanging on to Rajavi's coat tails. They still believe that the Mojahedin is a democratic force which will one day march into Tehran and take over the government of the country. So they stay by convincing themselves that their loyalty will be rewarded by a cabinet position or that they will be made head of an organisation. This of course, is promised to them by the organisation.

Some stay simply because they benefit more from being in the organisation than if they were out of it, or so they think. This is particularly so for women, especially those not from the educated middle class.

Why do women stay?

The Mojahedin's ideology presently gives complete precedence to women. This is a deliberately divisive policy, which throws men and women into conflict with one another rather than with the leader. Following a system which can be loosely described as 'positive discrimination', women are awarded positions of greater responsibility according to perceptions of their loyalty and men are expected to serve them regardless of any issue of competence. So much so, that the Leadership Council announced in 1993, which runs the Mojahedin organisation under Rajavi's guidance, consists solely of women.

In the Mojahedin, women are removed from their usual family context and roles. Basic needs are met, their food, clothing, shelter, sanitary facilities, child care – when the children were allowed to stay with them – and more are provided without them having to make extra time to provide these for themselves and possibly a family. Removing the responsibility of women for these menial tasks allows them to concentrate on other (also possibly menial) tasks, which they could not otherwise perform. This is part of a plan to force women – and men – to break down the mental barriers which they have built up all their lives in relation to gender specific activities. The women no longer have to work in the kitchen, and are asked to drive tanks instead. For most women this presents them with a huge mental leap into the dark about their own abilities. They have always seen themselves as, perhaps not physically weak, but certainly 'weak' in some indefinite, non-specific way that has never allowed them to even contemplate undertaking such a male specific role as driving a tank.

The view women and men have of themselves and their opposite gender, has always limited what each sex has chosen or allowed themselves to do. Once the traditional roles are removed and they are made to work outside them, this can be enormously liberating. For a mother of four children who married and bore them because that was all that her village life offered her, it can be close to a miracle to have this 'burden' removed from her and be allowed to take part in the challenges of army life. For a woman who has always been compared to her brothers as being stupid when placed against their academic success, it can be a massive revelation to her that she can successfully take charge of a whole department and run it efficiently.

However, it must be understood that these changes all come in a context of the individuals bearing no personal responsibility for their actions. Their orders come from above. If they fail to fulfil them, it is not seen as a failure to perform the task, but a failure of those involved to give total devotion to their leader.

There is nothing new in this idea of 'women's liberation'. Women in the West are also breaking these barriers to what a woman can do. It is happening in the armed forces, in business and in politics. But the majority of women, for whom these opportunities exist, choose not to abandon the family unit as the mainstay of their lives. This means that their struggle appears more protracted and diffuse, and it is hard to quantify what gains are being made.

In contrast, Mojahedin women who take up the challenge to break the mental gender barriers, although they appear to have succeeded in freeing themselves, are actually being exploited, not freed. It is a very subtle difference, but highly significant when the context is that of a cult. Mojahedin women are not given the choice of whether to have a family or not, this has been decided for them by Rajavi. Mojahedin members are expected to give one hundred percent obedience to the leaders and to obey their orders without question. This allows Rajavi to place women in positions of responsibility for which they have no competence. All they need to do is follow instructions. All the other members are required to obey them in turn.

Rajavi has sacrificed the efficiency of the work performed by his members, by making everyone submit to his requirements. The result is that a veteran with years of experience in any particular field, be it military, political or technical, is now expected to take orders from a woman who has no knowledge of the field. This might be acceptable if it was done for the benefit of the parties involved. But the woman is not expected to take instruction from the veteran to learn her job. As ever in the Mojahedin she must only take instruction from above because it is now the historical moment for women to free themselves from male domination. And the veteran is not required to obey the woman out of respect, but out of obedience to Rajavi who has declared that men must rid themselves of their gender bias toward women. The result of this blind obedience to changing the gender balance of power is that neither gender gains personally or changes themselves except to empty themselves of any ideas that might be interpreted as a challenge.

Rajavi throughout his career with the Mojahedin, has treated the members as disposable and dispensable, which has in fact always been part of the ideology. For the Mojahedin, those who sacrifice themselves are great and ten more will spring up to take their place. In itself, this is sad enough, but Rajavi's misuse of his followers' devotion shows a ruthless and cynical lack of humanity.

The first real example of Rajavi's propensity to sacrifice the lives of others was after the 30th Khordad or 20th June demonstration in 1981. Only the top members of the organisation were catered for with safe houses, arms and protection. Thousands of ordinary supporters were left to be wiped out by Khomeini's forces. There was no plan for failure and this has been a common theme. After Forouq – even the very fact of Forouq itself – there were no instructions for the troops on how to survive if they were injured, captured, or lost etc. The latest manifestation of this lack of care is in the terrorist units, which enter Iran to launch attacks and are caught by the regime's forces. They are given no education in how to survive prison, or interrogation, or even how to survive if they evade capture and become cut off from the organisation for weeks or even years. They are expected to blow themselves up or swallow cyanide tablets.

But this lack of care reveals itself also in the total inability for most of the members to live normal lives. Rajavi has robbed them of what all ordinary people have in the world, even those who live in hardship and poverty or under harsh repression or war, and that is freedom of thought.

Maryam's mission in Europe was to show Western women how the Mojahedin's ideology could free them. In my own experience the Mojahedin experiment has had an extremely narrowly defined success. The removal of women from their ordinary chores and concerns, including the care of children and the assignation of increasingly challenging tasks to perform in the army, has allowed those who were able, to break the mental barriers which all women have in all societies to varying degrees. The universal applicability of this experiment encouraged Rajavi to imagine he was God and could change the course of humankind, by taking the credit for liberating women. However, although his women members could possibly fight a war by commanding and operating tanks and artillery, etc, they could not survive for a day outside the protective environment of the organisation. This is Rajavi's crime against the women in the Mojahedin. He has freed them inside a cage, like freeing the potential of performing seals in the confines of a pool.

By depriving the Mojahedin members of the capacity to think critically and analytically, Rajavi has rendered them ridiculous as people. Such is the level of ignorance in which the members are kept that the women were afraid to wear second-hand clothes for fear that they would catch HIV/AIDS from the clothes. At the same time, the Iranian regime, which is scorned by these women, is conducting public education of both men and women in the dangers of unprotected sex and the use of shared needles in illegal drug usage. Women inside the repressive Iran of today still enjoy a greater freedom than any of the women in the Mojahedin.

For anyone joining at a later stage in the Ideological Revolution, the internal relations were for some time quite inaccessible. Even when told that it didn't matter at what point a person joined and that what mattered was to understand what was required, it was obvious that the people who had joined at the time of the revolution or before 1985, were in part of a process that had continued to the present day. Consequently you would need to have understood and accepted each part of this process in order to understand and accept what was going on now. What is interesting is that when the Internal Revolution was in full swing, this didn't seem to be a problem. No one seemed to care that a newcomer wasn't going to become indoctrinated, and no effort was put into bringing newcomers up to speed.

When the dust had settled after a couple of years, it became clear why this was so. It was because each and every person in the organisation was fighting just for his or her own existence. Members have to keep up with Rajavi's demands and these are not readily evident, they must guess them from the ones who have been in earlier neshasts. Then they must adapt themselves and make themselves believe in it and change and write reports to that effect. If they couldn't keep up to speed they would be hurled to the edges and perhaps even out of the organisation. So difficult was it for them all to come to terms with the requirements of each new phase, that they hadn't the knowledge, energy or ability to help anyone else to understand. It was as though they were all in a knock out contest. Anyone who didn't qualify would be knocked out at each stage. People became adept at pretending. It also became necessary to simply not think, to suspend critical analysis and in this way the organisation has taken on all the hallmarks of cult culture.

But curiously enough, it appears as though no one is masterminding this cult behaviour even though clearly Rajavi is. The whole Mojahedin culture has evolved inevitably out of Rajavi's demands on the members. In this way it has become both insidious and at the same time, patchy.

This situation has now changed. New members are required in order to show popular support and the Mojahedin are now actively recruiting. What they need are people who can be quite quickly indoctrinated. They have techniques, which they apply and those who are resistant are kept at arm's length until another issue arises or the person becomes more needy and so more susceptible to influence.

The Internal Revolution is both a tool of control and a response to internal dissent. Although Rajavi had lost ground in the international political scene, he kept on with his internal changes. Mostly this was due to the growing unease of members who could see that the goal of counter-revolution and marching on Tehran, was becoming a more and more distant dream. Some began to question the organisation in various ways and at various levels. The number of supporters in the West also began to decline. Year after year in the mass demonstrations held in major Western capitals and cities, the numbers decreased. Eventually, there could only ever be enough people if they were shipped in from other countries to make up sufficient numbers to gather in a salon or meeting hall. The Mojahedin membership has reduced drastically over the last ten years. The average age of the members is now over forty years old. As a cult leader, it is questionable how long Rajavi can continue to wear his emperor's new clothes.

Chapter 13

NATIONAL COUNCIL OF RESISTANCE

Since the early 1980s when the major players abandoned it, the National Council of Resistance of Iran has become more and more difficult to treat as a separate entity, independent of the Mojahedin. Certainly the leader of both the Mojahedin and the NCRI has remained the same unelected person, Massoud Rajavi. This chapter describes how the membership of both entities, becomes the same too.

Throughout the 1980s the opposition Labour Party and other socialist movements, gave unequivocal support to the NCRI in its struggle against the policies of the Iranian government. In strongly worded resolutions, successive Labour Conferences condemned the crimes of the Iranian government and backed the Iranian people's just resistance and their struggle for democracy. At that time, the NCRI was a coalition of opposition groups and personalities and the Mojahedin was only, on paper, one member. Each member had one vote on any policy issues and the right of veto. What the Labour Party and others recognised was that a strong resistance movement existed and should be encouraged. What was not clear, was just how quickly that resistance movement had been hijacked by Rajavi, and that the Iranian people's just resistance for democracy became his byword for Mojahedin activity and aims whatever these might be, democratic or not.

Rajavi's aims were never to establish democracy in Iran. He pitted himself against Khomeini at the start of the revolution in 1979, not as an advocate for power sharing, but like Khomeini himself, as someone who wanted 'everything or nothing'. Nowhere has Rajavi ever hinted that he has changed his ideas. What he has done, however, is to very cleverly field the NCRI as a cover for his real ideological aim. Where Khomeini was satisfied to impose Islamic rule on Iran at the point of the gun along with torture and execution, Rajavi sees no such limitation for himself. He sees his Islamic revolution as global. What is good for Iran is surely good for the world. Khomeini resisted pressure from his supporters to declare a jihad for all Muslims to defend the Islamic revolution in Iran. Where is the evidence to suggest that Rajavi could resist the same?

Bani Sadr left the NCRI because Rajavi made a peace treaty with Iraq during the eight-year war. Since then, Rajavi has become so deeply indebted to Saddam Hussein that he can refuse him nothing.

The Mojahedin in their document 'Unethical Policy' accuse the new Labour Government's Foreign Office, of betraying them. The Foreign Office however, had made it clear that they regarded the NCRI as a front for Rajavi's terrorism. With typical Mojahedin chutzpah, they ignored what had become obvious to everyone and attacked the Foreign Office for siding with the mullahs in Tehran. What they didn't explain is how the eleven member NCRI became diluted with over 500 Mojahedin members, each enjoying an individual vote, and why the NCRI supports, ratifies and condones the use of violence to achieve 'democratic' power in Iran.

For a long time, Rajavi saw the NCRI as a necessary evil, to be tolerated and worked around. Its members were an encumbrance and hindrance to his plans. He faced constant criticism of his plans and opposition to his moves. However, by 1985 when Rajavi was ready to impose the Ideological Revolution on Mojahedin members, he had created a sphere of manipulation, which allowed him to do so without too much opposition from the members. It didn't take him long to realise that, to a lesser degree, he could influence the NCRI members in a similar way. Once he had steered the NCRI through acceptance of his changes to the Mojahedin (which really had nothing to do with them) he set about manipulating them to accept his greater leadership.

After the Gulf War, Rajavi rapidly lost the confidence of his Western supporters. They began to regard him as a wild card, to be kept in the deck, but only to be played when things became desperate. As such, the West began to become more cautious in its various support, and that meant less support for the NCRI in their parliaments and senates. Fearing this loss of support, on 19th October 1991, eleven more members were added to the NCRI making it twenty-two strong. These were so-called personalities of the Resistance – politically motivated personalities who had shown themselves loyal to Rajavi. In reality the NCRI had shrunk because of the loss of Bani Sadr, the Kurdish Democratic Party and five more prominent members. These new members were only restoring what had already been lost.

On 28th December 1992, the NCRI was expanded from twenty-one to 150, to include some Mojahedin members. These Mojahedin members ceremoniously resigned from the Mojahedin in order to become individual members of the NCRI. But this didn't fool anyone. They still took their orders from Rajavi and were incapable of thinking or speaking for themselves. At the same time, Rajavi tried to get the NCRI to elect Maryam as President elect for the free Iran, but was forced to back off.

The atmosphere was not tolerant of him and his games. Since each member of the NCRI had a veto on policy, Rajavi still needed to convince the twenty-one non-Mojahedin members to accept his plans. Employing his usual methods of threats and blackmail, financial incentives, flattery and false promises, he managed to placate these members.

A year later he tried his luck again, and this time succeeded. In August 1993 the NCRI was expanded to 235 members and the number of Committees increased from eight to eighteen. The NCRI also adopted the Iranian Lion and Sun as its formal insignia; the emblem, which was used by the late Shah, but now with the crown removed from the Lion's head. As the crowning glory of this achievement, Rajavi also had the NCRI elect Maryam as 'Iran's President for the transitional period'. A role Rajavi had previously fought so hard to gain for himself when the NCRI was first established in 1981. Maryam was taken out of her army uniform and dressed in expensive civilian clothes. Her image was rejigged and this new presidential style presented in glossy magazines was distributed widely to Western political channels.

In preparation for promoting Maryam from her role as leader of the Mojahedin, on 10th August 1993 Rajavi had the organisation elect a Leadership Council. This consisted of twelve members – harking back to the original Mojahedin structure – with a further twelve deputies. Significantly, all of these twenty-four were women, all loyal to Rajavi and all elected in an open session in which a yes or no vote was recorded for each candidate. Each one received a one hundred per cent 'yes' vote. Then, when Maryam's new role of President elect for the NCRI was created, it meant that neither Rajavi nor Maryam were officially in charge of the Mojahedin. So, Rajavi also had the organisation elect Fahimeh Arvani as Secretary General of the Mojahedin. She was subsequently replaced by a rapid succession of other women. Fahimeh and the Leadership Council declared their allegiance to Maryam. Under their command, the whole Mojahedin would be at her service as the NCRI's President elect. Well, why wouldn't they? All that had happened was that Rajavi had co-opted the NCRI to be part of the Mojahedin and presented it in the reverse.

What had concerned Rajavi for some time, was that in Iran there was a non-elected Supreme Leader and an elected President. Feeling insecure, he decided to replicate this structure in the Iranian Resistance movement (as he called his opposition of the Islamic Republic). He had already done this internally after the defeat of Forouq and the next phase of the Ideological Revolution, placing Maryam nominally in charge and announcing himself the ideological leader. Now he created an 'elected' President in order to show to the outside world that he is above normal politics. His role was that of non-elected

Supreme Leader though he only referred to himself as the spiritual leader.

The fundamental reason for this new development of the NCRI was that Rajavi desperately needed to rebuild his contact with the West. He couldn't do this directly himself as none of the Western countries would accept him whilst he continued to maintain relations with Saddam. Nor would Saddam let him loose to leave Iraq and do what he wanted beyond his control. Rajavi hoped that by presenting Maryam as a President and giving her over 150 devoted members to choose from, she could go to the West and start building a place for him again in the political scene. It became a costly mistake. Maryam, as good as she was at promoting Rajavi for the members of the Mojahedin, could not act as a good CEO and take advice. She ignored the experience and advice of the members already in the West and came up with her own ideas. Her ability to promote Rajavi was solely in the circumstances of a camp in Iraq with no TV or newspapers or books, in fact no outside contact at all for the members.

Maryam was not a political person, neither did she have much experience in the world. She had been trained for years to do what she was doing for Rajavi, and had no ideas beyond this. Because of this, when she arrived in Europe in October 1993, she immediately set about paying the expenses for European and American feminists to visit her in Paris. Once there, they listened to her concept of a global women's movement under the ideological leadership of Rajavi and herself which would free Western women, unfortunately forgetting in the meantime to put aside her Muslim headscarf (hijab)!

She did not see or grasp the change of scene among Iranians in the West either. When Rajavi had left Paris in 1986, he had published a video of his speech in which he stressed emphatically that the legitimacy of any opposition's stay in the West had ended because this legitimacy only existed at all due to his forces carrying out armed operations inside Iran. He broke off all his ties with the West including his own supporters (who still remained loyal). When the Mojahedin came back with Maryam, the supporters were shocked by their behaviour. In the same way that Rajavi had put himself beyond the reach of ordinary members of the Mojahedin by creating Maryam and Fahimeh and then the Leadership Council as a buffer, now the ordinary members did the same thing in relation to the unsuspecting supporters. The members, including Maryam who was preaching her Ideological Revolution to Western women, saw themselves as superior beings to the supporters. They thought that the hardship that they were going through was a different experience compared to the lives of ordinary people and that this somehow gave them superior status. This was just the same as Rajavi's approach in relation to the ordinary members. In reality it seemed that even the most educated and experienced members, after fifteen years in the isolation of the camps in Iraq, had become little more than villagers in their mentality and behaviour, never mind the actual villagers among them who were illiterate and unworldly.

Even the most idiotic of the Mojahedin now felt that it was their right and duty to lord it above the supporters. They issued commands and acted in the most overbearing manner. This was both ludicrous (how can you take someone seriously when they command you to switch the contents of the salt and pepper pots for the dinner table), but it was also desperately sad. The supporters had to refuse to do these things because no rational human being would allow his or herself to be treated in such a humiliating and demeaning fashion. Particularly since they had made so many sacrifices in their own lives to remain loyal to the Mojahedin's struggle.

And yet it was clear that the irony of the situation did not occur to the members. They simply couldn't understand this reluctance to obey. They rationalised and justified it by telling themselves that the supporters simply didn't understand. They had not made the ideological leap of faith and had not committed themselves to the leader as they had. They simply thought that Rajavi was right all along. No one, except the few rare Mojahedin members, could possibly grasp the enormity of the revolution and its implications. The fact that those perfectly devoted and committed supporters were now unable to work with them, held no meaning other than this. In fact it was only the tolerance and devotion of the supporters which allowed the deception to continue as it did. It was they who found a way to work alongside these great beings, the Mojahedin from Iraq.

An example of this was in Iran Aid where the reigning champion money grabbers, Susan, Siavosh, Ashraf and others, were ignominiously cast into the shadows by these new non-English speaking members, who were able, through their bullying tactics, to pocket between £1,000 to £2,000 per day for the Mojahedin. This was three times the previous amount. In spite of their previous ascendancy the supporters had to back down and accept their lesser place in the scheme of things.

Background to Maryam's 'promotion' and visit to Europe

Maryam was to be sent to Paris for one reason and that was to win back the ground lost in the international political scene. How difficult or possible this may have been needs analysis beyond the scope of this book, but let us look at what they envisaged and what they actually did.

Internationally, Rajavi has been questioned many times about the same issues: What is your stance toward Iraq in its invasion of Kuwait? What is your position about the Iraqi use of chemicals against Iranians and against the Iraqi Kurds, and Saddam's propensity to kill even the people closest to him if he suspects they are not loyal enough? How are you being financed, including arms?

Rajavi's answer has always been 'Give me a better place to fight Khomeini and I will move.' The exact meaning of this is 'Give me the equivalent or better than I already have, then I will give up what Saddam is providing for me'. The propaganda machine of the Mojahedin implies that whatever losses the Mojahedin have suffered, have been sacrificed for Rajavi. For example, that he has paid the price with 30th Khordad, Forouq and the sacrifice of his brother, sister, wife, friends and comrades. But if we look carefully behind all this propaganda, it is clear that Rajavi has never accepted to give or risk anything personally or politically, and perhaps this is true of every dictator whether in power or not.

Rajavi is very good at spending from other people's pockets, especially in using the deaths of his followers. In his words, 'Forouq insured the Mojahedin' which meant that the blood of the people killed on both sides would prevent any moderation in any way for a long time to come. Of course, this is true and the more killing in any conflict the stronger the hardliners become on both sides. The more hatred is engendered, the less possibility there is for reforming or moderating activities to take place.

Even putting aside the loss of people and ignoring any issues of morality within a power struggle, it is still clear that there are other areas of a political struggle in which it is impossible not to take a risk, i.e. no risk, no win. Rajavi has never accepted this unless he has seen that what he might lose, has gone anyway. This has been revealed very clearly in the case of Iraq. Rajavi will not give up Saddam, but still wants the support of the West, which of course is unacceptable for everybody. When pushed for an answer, Rajavi says 'give me double and then I'll leave'. He doesn't understand that he must say 'I will prove myself and earn my respect by leaving and then asking for help', which is usually the way life is conducted, personally or politically. (Imagine a marriage – husband to wife: 'take me back and then I'll give up my mistress!')

Covering his bets was also the name of his game at the time of the revolution; contacting Western countries and Arab states while at the same time maintaining a close relationship with the Soviet Union. This may have worked in the short term, but in the long run, obviously everybody will leave you, both Iranian and non-Iranian, and you end up with a few thousand people in a camp under Saddam Hussein's supervision. Remember that according to his own words, Rajavi called upon half a million people at two hour's notice to support him during 30th Khordad.

A further look at the controversy of Rajavi's political history shows an unprincipled avoidance of risk. The Mojahedin is an anti-imperialist group with a history of killing Americans, now happily having petitions signed by American Senators in 1991 while they stayed in Iraq. These Senators quickly withdrew their signatures when they discovered what they had been hoodwinked into supporting. The Mojahedin is a Muslim group with historical ties with the PLO, seeking the support of the Jewish lobby in the United States against the Iranian regime, and at the same time holding meetings with Yassir Arafat. The Mojahedin fought for Saddam in the Gulf War and at the same time took money from Saudi Arabia. Both the Jewish lobby and Saudi Arabia have now stopped any support. The Mojahedin have their main base in Paris, but at the same time threatened the French during the Gabon crisis with suicide bombings.

Perhaps most damaging of all was the Mojahedin's role during the Iran–Iraq War when they were effectively helping the Iraqi war effort while claiming to be fighting for the people of Iran. The Mojahedin still provide intelligence for the Iraqis about Iran as part of their deal for Iraqi support. A lot of false information is also passed to Western countries through their security services, while at the same time, the Mojahedin have never offered one iota of intelligence about Iraq to Western governments.

Further examples of how the Mojahedin cheat and lie and give false information in their relations with the West are as follows. The Mojahedin bought tickets for a charity dinner in the USA, and sent their representative to shake hands with President Clinton who had attended as guest of honour. They subsequently published a photograph of the forced handshake, describing it as a personal meeting. At the same time, the Mojahedin boldly requested a radio licence from America to broadcast their propaganda. The Mojahedin have also habitually obtained the designated two passes to attend the British Labour Party Conference and then by giving the passes to others, made sure that about ten or more members got into the conference hall to undertake lobbying.

With this background, the Mojahedin left Paris and went to Baghdad. Rajavi is now imprisoned in Iraq, but has tried to revert everything back to how it was, by sending Maryam to Europe without paying a political penny.

Maryam's attempt to win back Western support

Maryam was brought out of Iraq in 1993 with their approval, but without informing the French, as the Mojahedin were afraid that France would prevent her entry. They told the Jordanians that she was going, but they didn't say where. The French reluctantly accepted her as an asylum seeker, but the security they provided did not have the flashing lights as it had before Rajavi left Paris. They refused to close the road in front of her residence as they had done before and they refused other privileges such as the telephones and free electricity, which they had also given before. In effect she was received as an ordinary asylum seeker except where they suspected there might be an assassination attempt. As for meetings, they insisted that she keep a low profile and that is one reason why Maryam had to go to Dortmund and Earls Court in London for public appearances.

In order to pursue her 'presidential' role and establish a political identity, Maryam started holding meetings for the NCRI, trying to copy whatever she had seen from Rajavi. But every time the meetings ended up as conference calls with Baghdad, as the non-Mojahedin members who still remained in the NCRI, didn't accept her as their Chairman (let alone as President). Maryam didn't have the authority to do anything without asking Rajavi.

In a matter of weeks she gave up on this and distanced herself from the NCRI by asking them to form more Committees and to follow various programmes and report back on them. They were unable to do this of course, because all of the money and the workforce brought from Iraq were in the hands of Maryam. Instead, Maryam privately instructed her followers to pursue the Mojahedin's Ideological Revolution and internationalise it. To this day, it is unclear whether Rajavi had total knowledge about Maryam's change of strategy, or whether she had just assumed that when he said no he meant yes, as in previous phases of the Ideological Revolution.

Meanwhile, in Iraq, Rajavi had started another phase of the Ideological Revolution, the phase of freeing yourself from yourself and surrendering your minds and thoughts to the leader, dubbed by former members as the 'Khar' (donkey) phase.

Maryam wanted to keep up with that also, but forgot that the members in Iraq are first of all under complete control and isolated and secondly, they didn't have any real job to do. The result was tragic.

Maryam began her new strategy of internationalising the Ideological Revolution by holding meetings for women. She paid for people to come and be her audiences. She began to pay monthly salaries to lobby groups only for them to send some third rate, retired political celebrity to be photographed with her. She organised dinner dance programmes and paid popular Iranian singers four times their normal fees (knowing they would lose their current audiences in Los Angeles). Some she even persuaded to be on the NCRI payroll as she thought this might change her luck and attract people, obviously forgetting that she was still supposed to be a Muslim revolutionary who does not shake hands with men, who wears the hijab and doesn't drink alcohol. Later on, any of these singers who had not just kept away in the first place, where they could still make money independently, returned to their previous audiences. They apologised to the Iranians in Los Angeles in radio programmes and begged their forgiveness.

Maryam made several videos with these singers from the time of the Shah. She posed as if she were Farah Diba, wife of the late Shah, under the flag of Iran with the Lion and Sun. This reminded people of the good old days of the Shah with the difference that anyone who wanted these good old days, didn't need the Mojahedin. Living in the West, wealthy and influential expatriate Iranians could recreate the atmosphere much better than she could. The only people she attracted were a rag bag of poor, lower class refugees who were fooled into thinking that this was indeed a recreation of a past which they had never enjoyed in the first place and was now being offered to them at a discount. The result of all this was not to make Maryam more popular among Iranians, but rather to leave her entourage, mostly the members she brought from Iraq, more confused than ever. Remember that they had already become confused when they conflicted with the ordinary supporters of the Mojahedin who couldn't accept their high-handed ways and told them in no uncertain terms where to get off. Now they had to organise and attend dinner dances for the hoi polloi. Members started leaving. This started with the ones who had somewhere to go, those who had relatives living outside Iran with whom they could find refuge. Others followed, asking the French officials for help, in finding them lodging and social security.

Marzieh joins the NCRI

During this time, the singer Marzieh had come from Iran to visit friends in Europe. Her friends had contact with the Mojahedin and informed them of her visit. The Mojahedin saw this as an excellent opportunity. They did everything possible to keep her, and as a famous singer of the Shah's time, she couldn't resist this renewed attention. She was allotted three people, twenty-four hours a day, seven days a week, to provide whatever she wanted. She was given a house with a purpose built recording studio in Paris. The Mojahedin paid for her to sing at the Albert Hall in London. She was made Head of the Cultural Committee of the NCRI, replacing Dr Hezarkhani, who along with the Matine Daftarys, was the only reputable person left in the NCRI. Hedayat and Maryam Matine Daftary had resisted the changes in the NCRI and were hoping to change the NCRI to a democratic organisation with an influx of these new personalities. They resigned from the NCRI only a few months later.

Maryam's various approaches to gain Western political support were being rejected on two grounds. Firstly, that she didn't have any support inside Iran and secondly that she didn't have any support outside Iran either. For this reason, she was desperate to show some crowds outside Iran, and Rajavi was desperate to show some action inside Iran. He started sending terrorist teams back inside. However, even in this he was thwarted. By Saddam on one side and by the continual arrests of his teams on the other side. This of course, was due to the infiltration of his organisation and the intelligence reaching the Iranian regime.

Maryam's efforts were in the form of music concerts and dinner dances. At one point, in Dortmund, to save face, she had supporters brought from all over America and Europe, and even paid for German groups to come and fill the salon. She had no understanding that what her critics in the West meant was not propaganda and concerts, they meant supporters as in political supporters willing to accept the Mojahedin as a political alternative or at least as an opposition to the current regime. For the West, Rajavi was a burned card who had stubbornly lost his historical chances, and Maryam they assessed, with a few upgrades, would remain an idealistic head of the feminist movement of a third world country's exiled group.

It didn't take long, no more than a few months, for everyone to realise the dimensions of the failure of Maryam's efforts. All their efforts and Iraqi money had brought them an even worse situation than they started with. The description of 'Iraqi money' is used because Rajavi has to report to Saddam what he has been doing, while Iraq provides all their resources. After Maryam returned to Iraq, Rajavi desperately tried to undertake some military activities in order to gain favour with Saddam again, but even this failed. Not only have no doors been opened in the West, the Mojahedin are becoming increasingly unwanted. First, France started giving hints that Maryam should leave. This came as a warning by France that they would have to reduce the level of security provided for her, as they didn't see the same threat from the regime as before and they needed their forces in more important places. This could have been because of assurances from the Iranians that they wouldn't be pursuing this avenue.

Meanwhile from the other side, the Iranian community outside Iran had a less than welcome message for them. Some had boycotted them altogether and some would take advantage of the free trips and tickets for the concerts and dinner dances which were arranged in various cities, but they wouldn't give any actual support, either in terms of time or finance. It was obvious that no matter how many events they arranged in various cities or countries, they were never going to get enough people to attend a demonstration as a show of support. Not only that, but on a daily basis Maryam was losing the members who had been brought from Iraq in an attempt to gather support and supporters, and it was just a matter of time before the whole organisation dissolved.

Maybe it was these pressures that finally brought her – or him – to their senses. However, it was by now too late to rescue the situation by arranging a political show of support. Maryam quickly went to Norway to speak in City Hall in Oslo. She then visited London. But Britain only granted her a visa after making sure they had a written guarantee from France that she would be able to return there. Clearly once she arrived in England, she would try to stay, and the French would have been more than happy to be rid of her. Maryam tried in these last few months to make approaches all over Europe, but she wasn't accepted. Britain was the face saving trip; in so much as they had any face left to save. Britain reluctantly accepted that they would not prevent the Mojahedin from gathering supporters from all over the world for the Earls Court concert. Shortly after, Lord Avebury agreed to arrange a meeting in the Houses of Parliament using his influence there as a humanitarian, but this failed to attract many people and none of note or influence came.

Earls Court

The concert to be held at Earls Court, London in July 1985 was announced as a concert for Marzieh. There was no mention of Maryam's arrival in Britain or her intention to give a speech. Supporters suspected that this was planned, but this made no difference to the overall approach to the event. Many had become tired of the Mojahedin calling in the supporters and announcing a 'bassij' (all out effort), setting the targets higher and higher. It began to look pointless and desperate. Only those supporters who had a vested interest in continuing their support (usually because of financial benefit) carried on pretending to go along with these schemes. Most were simply cynical and on this occasion, many left feeling this really was the last straw. Quite simply, the supporters saw nothing in any of these activities which looked like an adequate response to the situation inside Iran.

When Maryam did arrive at the concert hall, many still believed that she had merely come to watch. When she walked onto the stage to speak, flanked by two British Security agents, many Iranians walked out in protest. These were ordinary Iranians who had no wish to be involved in politics and absolutely no wish at all to be associated in any way with the Mojahedin. They had come because of their past admiration of Marzieh and hoped only to hear her sing the old songs.

Many non-Iranians had also been duped into attending too. Thousands of free tickets had been distributed to the Salvation Army (with the request that they not wear their uniforms as this was a social occasion), and other charities for the homeless. Afghan asylum seekers were visited in their hostels and pressurised into attending in an attempt to fill the salon. All these people were told that this was a Persian cultural event and that Marzieh was especially inviting them. When people arrived at Earls Court to go in, there was a large picture of Marzieh at the entrance. But when people left, an even bigger picture of Maryam had replaced this, in order to take pictures for propaganda purposes.

Marzieh's son, who was on his way to America, had stopped in Britain to see his mother. Finding no other way to gain access to his mother, he approached her while she was on the stage. He was dragged aside and in front of the audience, severely beaten up by Maryam's Mojahedin bodyguards. Later he published a leaflet entitled *'Mama, sing, but only for the people of Iran'*. The Mojahedin denied that they had wanted to prevent him from speaking to his mother. They claimed that they didn't know he was her son when they saw him shouting to his mother on the stage. But this was completely untrue, they knew exactly who he was and had anticipated his actions.

The day following Earls Court, Maryam held a smaller meeting for 'close supporters', that is, those who had been brought from every other Western country and had their trips paid for them from as far afield as Australia, the United States and Canada. By halfway through Maryam's speech, about a third of this audience had left the salon and gone off for sight seeing or shopping or other things they had planned. So much for cashing in on the success of the previous night's concert.

As well as this concert and meeting, Maryam paid out huge expenses, including renting an expensive office suite in Westminster, in an attempt to show her prestige. None of these things worked. She went back to Paris to pack her bags. In autumn 1995 Maryam returned to Iraq leaving behind about thirty percent of the people who had come from Iraq with her and who had left the organisation while they could.

The NCRI was depleted, and with the lowest possible morale. All the money was spent paying for concerts, supporters' airfares and hotels, and useless lobbying organisations. Some of these promised a meeting with Margaret Thatcher, but none delivered. Instead, Maryam met with Yassir Arafat who had a lecture engagement at Oxford University. And he only agreed to meet with her on the basis of knowing the founders of the Mojahedin and those who had trained in the PLO camps in the late 1960s.

Maryam returns to Iraq empty handed

On Maryam's return to Iraq, the Mojahedin desperately tried to show some action inside Iran and to make themselves known as a threat to the regime, especially for Saddam who was providing all their facilities. But there was too much infiltration or the regime's intelligence was simply too good. All these attempts ended in failure with the arrest or killing of the teams. The Mojahedin managed eventually to send one mortar bomb into an office compound in Tehran and one into a residential area, also in Tehran.

In the middle of this crisis currently facing the Mojahedin, the regime itself was beginning to make huge advances in international relations under the election of the new President Khatami. Khatami's doctrine of critical dialogue was gaining increasing momentum and thereby changing the West's policy of sanctions and hostility and trying to overthrow the regime into a policy of changing it from within. It was not long before Western governments began to cold shoulder the Mojahedin.

Note on the National Council of Resistance

Although it became obvious very early on, after the removal of Bani Sadr, that Rajavi wasn't serious about the NCRI, it is still worth looking at it briefly to show its total lack of credibility or relevance.

National – it has never been an umbrella for all Iranian opposition forces, nor has it ever enjoyed the majority support of the nation.

Council – There have never been independent views, which have challenged each other.

Resistance – Means that they should resist some kind of unpopular actions or ideas. But the Mojahedin believes in an Islamic Republic with Rajavi as its sole head. This is hardly what people want if the regime changes.

Iran – The Mojahedin have had no presence inside Iran for at least the past fifteen years, and can no longer claim to be 'of Iran'.

Part Three
The Mojahedin in the Present

Chapter 14

DISSENT WITHIN THE MOJAHEDIN

This book had tried to show how and why Massoud Rajavi has perverted the Mojahedin organisation for his own aims. His primary aim throughout has been to achieve power in Iran through violence. That is, without reference to any political process. Rajavi wants 'either everything or nothing'. So far he has been denied any involvement in Iranian politics except as the perpetrator of terrorist acts in the country. In order to fulfil his aim, Rajavi has put the Mojahedin organisation through a most extraordinary series of changes. This chapter seeks to examine the impact of those changes on the members.

With the 1985 announcement of the Ideological Revolution, Massoud Rajavi engineered an ideological coup on the organisation. Although it started life as a politically ideological and revolutionary organisation, Rajavi changed the Mojahedin out of all recognition. It is now operating around a pseudo-religious ideology for which Rajavi is the deity. Was the change necessary? Did they have to change in order to survive? It is possible to argue that any organisation has a degree of organic and dynamic change built into it. Also, that it must be flexible enough to make pragmatic alterations to the way it operates as a consequence of both the world it exists in and the demands of the situation it is in direct relation to.

But the Mojahedin has done almost the opposite of what could have been expected. Rather than change in response to external demands, the organisation has wilfully ignored these and instead, obeying its own internal dynamic, rendered itself more and more distant from any constituency it might possibly have previously had recourse to for support. This internal dynamic is controlled directly by Rajavi himself and it demands that the organisation, down to every last member, must be kept totally and unquestioningly obedient to him.

One highly significant, but overlooked aspect of the Mojahedin's internal status, is that the vast majority of its members comprise the original membership of before the 1979 revolution up to 1985 when recruitment changed. These are what Maryam Rajavi refers to as 'Massoud's generation'. It gives an average age to the organisational members of between forty-five and fifty years. This alone makes it impossible to regard the Mojahedin as an ordinary fighting force. Certainly it is not a force, which can take on the Iranian armed forces. However, it is a force, which is prepared to sacrifice itself in such a way that makes it just as useful to Rajavi in the long term. These members are in it 'to the end'. For them, ordinary life holds no attraction or meaning. Indeed one of the Mojahedin's pejorative terms about their supporters is that they are 'ordinary people'.

Those who have met them might indeed say that they are not ordinary people. Members of the Mojahedin exude a kind of attractive purity and intensity of purpose, which on the surface appears as a deep personal confidence and conviction. Their behaviour, however, is the result of having lost all their inhibitions and having no personal responsibility for anything or toward anyone beyond obedience to Rajavi. Their existence is completely outside what is recognisable as normal experience. The normal values, which govern any society, have no meaning for the Mojahedin. The values of honesty, truth, independent thought, freedom of action to name but a few, have no meaning here.

The key to understanding this extraordinary situation is to go beyond the Mojahedin's professed political platform and examine the behaviour of the organisation toward its own members. Since the inception of the Ideological Revolution,

Rajavi has exerted more and more control over every aspect of the members' lives. In 1985 Rajavi called for living martyrs. This allowed him to order his followers to do what he asked of them beyond the normal range of political or revolutionary tasks which it might be thought necessary for overthrowing the Iranian regime. Such acts included forced marriages. In particular, after operation Forouq-e Javidan in 1988 in which many members lost a spouse or other family member. Although it was introduced as maintaining family values, it was clearly about testing and rewarding loyalty. In particular a trend began to appear among women who were 'given' a husband. Those who were most devoted to Rajavi began to reject their husbands according to Maryam's example, that is, Maryam's rejection of her own husband Mehdi Abrishamchi to marry with her ideological equal, Rajavi. None of this was ever spoken. Indeed much of the Mojahedin ideology is planted, grown and perpetuated simply by example and peer pressure.

This led on to the next stage in the Ideological Revolution. In 1990 Rajavi required everyone to divorce. He gave Abrishamchi as the example. He said that Abrishamchi had divorced his wife and accepted that she marry Rajavi because of his understanding of the ideological necessity for it. Now all the members were required to understand and make this sacrifice. The women should consider themselves as belonging to Rajavi and the men should accept this and lay no claim to any woman. This involved non-married members also. It was meant as an ideological commitment to Rajavi, rather than as the physical separation of the sexes, although this was fundamental to it too. And Rajavi had no intention of laying claim to the women except as forces to work for him.

Then in 1994, whilst Maryam was in Europe, Rajavi instigated a series of meetings in which he demanded the hearts and minds of the members. They were required to individually submit to a kind of ritual public humiliation and thereby show that they had fully submitted every aspect of themselves to Rajavi. Members had to divest themselves of every vestige of pride. Pride, that sense of individualism everyone possesses, would in Rajavi's view, allow them to form opinions and concepts outside those he wanted them to have.

The most recent development has been described as 'ideological Qosl'. Qosl is the ritual washing of the whole body, which gives Muslims the necessary state of cleanliness for praying. Rajavi currently requires his members to perform a kind of ritual ideological cleansing. This must be done once a week in public and on camera. He is no longer satisfied with the daily reports. People must now have no way to hide or disguise themselves.

This behaviour in an organisation is extraordinary. It is questionable whether members of a political organisation could allow themselves to be so treated. However, this strange situation begins to make sense when viewed within the framework of what constitutes a cult. Then it becomes clear why the Mojahedin behave like this and why the organisation is rejected by most right thinking Iranians and reviled by almost all ex-members.

Rajavi cannot possibly have set out to create a cult no matter how convenient such a structure has become for him. His first ambitions were political and he wanted not a share in power in Iran, but power over all the country. This book describes the actual progress of his failure in that respect and how the choices made by Rajavi, irrevocably skewed the future of the organisation. Rajavi clearly wanted power and was prepared to subordinate the whole organisation and all its members into a means for him to achieve this. However, what is startling to observe, is that at some imperceptible point, the organic culture of the organisation took on a life of its own and the slide into a cult could not be stopped or diverted, even had the leader wanted to. Well, so long as it is in his favour why should he want to?

So what is a cult?

In *Cults: A Practical Guide* written by Ian Haworth of the Cult Information Centre, there is a definition of a cult as an entity having the following five characteristics:

1. It uses psychological coercion to recruit, indoctrinate and retain its members.
2. It forms an elitist totalitarian society.
3. Its founder or leader is self-appointed, dogmatic, messianic, not accountable and has charisma.
4. It believes 'the end justifies the means' in order to solicit funds, recruit people and, in this case, to further its political ends.
5. Its wealth does not benefit its members or society.

The Mojahedin fit all these characteristics. But Ian Haworth goes on to describe the problems with cult culture as follows:

Why are cults harmful?

He states that to remain within the strict mental and social confines of a cult for even a short time can have the following disastrous effects:

1. Loss of choice and free will.
2. Diminished intellectual ability, vocabulary and sense of humour.
3. Reduced use of irony, abstractions and metaphors.
4. Reduced capacity to form flexible and intimate relationships.
5. Poor judgement.
6. Physical deterioration.
7. Malnutrition.
8. Hallucinations, panic, dissociation, guilt, identity diffusion and paranoia.
9. Neurotic, psychotic or suicidal tendencies.

The greatest concerns then as regards the Mojahedin are firstly, that membership of any cult is damaging to the mental, physical and emotional health of all its members. In addition, membership of this particular cult deprives the person of every basic human right as defined in the Universal Declaration of Human Rights. (Which the Mojahedin claims to uphold in its denunciation of the regime's crimes.) In this respect there are two areas of concern. One is for existing members who are ignorant of the damage they are inflicting on themselves and the other is for those who reject the cult and more importantly its leader. Let us first look at the conditions encountered by the willing members.

Obedience

The proper term which is used in the Mojahedin is 'submission' to Massoud's will. But this is likely to give an impression that the people involved are weak. Yet there is nothing weak about a person who is willing to perform any task, including dying, for their belief. Obedience better expresses Rajavi's use of these people and so it is this, rather than submission, which must head this description of what it, is like to be inside the Mojahedin.

A fundamental question surrounding this issue of obedience is to ask why would a reasonably intelligent person not only allow his or herself to be so manipulated, but to also take part in the self-policing of this manipulation to such a point that it drives some of them insane? Why do people accept such all encompassing control over every aspect of their lives that is used in the Mojahedin? Aside from the use of psychological manipulation or 'brainwashing', the simplest explanation is that Rajavi's cult is that most dangerous of all cults, for its members and the world at large, that is, a cult with a just cause to fight. No matter at what phase of the internal relations, the organisation has recruited and continues to recruit members, however few, on the basis of a just cause. That is, the struggle against religious dictatorship in Iran. It is a nationalistic, political and religious struggle with a broad appeal, and it was, and perhaps remains, a genuine cause.

To maintain this position members are fed a constant diet of misinformation. One of the first acts of Rajavi after the Ideological Revolution was to ban people from reading books, or accessing any other external information source. This worked easily even among the 'diplomacy' section whose personnel naturally had reason to access every kind of media in their line of work. When organisations such as Amnesty International were dismissed by the top leaders as biased and not to be trusted, then ordinary newspapers and media programmes were unquestionably unreliable. This allowed the members who could access them to treat them with disdain and to not want to seek news or opinion from these sources. Moreover, the work of actually monitoring these media was transferred to the supporters whose own opinions and ideas were already treated with an unspoken contempt by the members.

Inside Iraq itself, there was no opportunity to access any other information than that which was broadcast in the daily news bulletin and the closed circuit television programmes created by the Mojahedin for internal consumption. Among Western observers who receive the Mojahedin's accounts of human rights abuses in Iran, there is scepticism due to the blatant exaggeration behind their claims. But the Mojahedin members believe these 'facts' and this motivates them to ever greater sacrifices for their leader.

Fairly soon after the Ideological Revolution, Rajavi implied more and more that members should not interfere with politics and should only try to correct themselves ideologically and perform their allotted tasks as they are expected to do them. They were to be ready to sacrifice everything for him because he represents the 'big bank' of the revolution and their sacrifices will be spent wisely by him and him alone.

Rajavi's idea of democracy has always been that everybody has the chance of choosing a leader once in their life. As far as he is concerned, people chose either him or Khomeini. After that, the responsibility lay only with the leader, not the individual. People should have no moral guilt if they are totally obedient to the leader. Therefore, good and bad are not for the individual to decide. Members are not even responsible before God because the leader has sacrificed himself to take all their responsibility before God.

Later Rajavi implied in his speeches that if such a leader has done his job well enough, then he starts a relationship with the Imam Zaman (the last and still awaited Imam in Shiite Islam) and therefore has direct contact with God. He brought examples from Prophet Mohammad and compared himself to the Shiite Imams. The result of this was to create a mentality of complete lack of responsibility, which would allow the person to take part in suicide bombings or Forouq-e Javidan or any other actions.

After the Internal Revolution, members were required to write about their relationship with their spouse and children, and to report dreams and in fact any thoughts they had at all, good or bad. They were told to write about their sexual relationship with their spouse. All this information, even though the writer might have felt it was innocuous, was going to be used against them. For Rajavi, if someone had a happy, well-adjusted and positive relationship with their spouse and children this was a disaster. It meant that the person didn't need him, and this would lead the person to question his leadership. He would confront such a person with the challenge that they were thinking wrongly.

The confusion caused to such a person could and has tipped the balance of a person's mind. There have been several instances in which the mental pressure a person imposes on themselves to make sense of the hideously contorted version of reality which he is forced to accept has forced some to commit suicide. Others have relinquished control of their minds completely and succumbed to psychotic illness. Several of these individuals can be found in psychiatric hospitals in Baghdad.

For everyone else, all these various stages of the Ideological Revolution resulted in members deceiving themselves and fabricating lies about themselves, to themselves. These people reached a happy state of self-delusion in which it became obvious to them and to everyone else that whenever they have a thought, it has been against the interests and benefit of Rajavi. Therefore, by accepting this in their heart, they should merely work like a machine and try their best not to allow themselves to think or have ideas.

It is clear also that some members are playing a game, and don't believe in what they are doing, but merely masquerade for convenience. There must be a state of constant vigilance for members to make sure they are doing the right thing and won't be found lacking.

The generic term is psychological manipulation. But this is something which can only with the greatest difficulty be specified or confronted by the person who is undergoing it. It is a deliberately elusive practice. People are made to understand things through the behaviour of those around them. For instance, a simple technique is to ignore a person until they understand that they should work harder and engage more in taking instruction. Ignoring a person makes them feel needy of others. Of course this works very well in the extremely sociable Iranian culture. But, wherever there did appear to be a danger that the person would take umbrage and walk away, allowance was made and a sympathetic massul would kindly attend to the person's mood to placate and guide them back to the right path; unquestioning obedience.

This individual attention to each and every member takes a huge amount of energy from the organisation. But they regard it as necessary and advertise it inside themselves as being part of their ideological duty to guide people in understanding the greatness that is Rajavi. In reality, the Mojahedin are hugely inefficient for this reason, and this diversion of energy from the real struggle into internal control, has been one of the major factors in preventing their growth and progress.

It is difficult to actually define the belief system which governs the Mojahedin. Certainly it has nothing to do with politics, or even religion for that matter. In the end it doesn't really matter what the members believe because Rajavi demands that they deny their own thoughts and simply obey his commands.

Little by little, after the Ideological Revolution, the Mojahedin gave up reading the Qoran and other religious books, such as the Nahjol Balaqa etc. Then they began to give up religious practices, such as prayers and fasting. They had been instructed in the ideology that now they had chosen an ideological leader, they were no longer individually responsible. Rajavi's message was that they were only responsible to him and it is he who is responsible to God.

With this message in their hearts, some members were left with a dilemma when they came to the West with Maryam. In particular, those who had come from a liberal and middle class family background, and had perhaps been educated in a university in a Western country. These members more easily succumb to the temptation to revert to the values and lifestyle they had previously enjoyed. This giving in to their wanting to do things which Islam forbids, came from the point of view that they no longer believed that they were responsible for their ideas, this was all taken up by Rajavi as their ideological leader. On this basis they had justified in their own minds the suicide bombings, terrorism, giving up spouses and children, begging in streets for money, cheating social security systems, cheating western politicians, and working with Saddam Hussein's regime, including giving intelligence to him. In relation to all these things, eating pork or not saying prayers, or shaking hands with a member of the opposite sex, seemed quite innocuous.

Rajavi's contradiction was that he could not give up the benefits of being Muslim in an Iranian environment, or an Iraqi environment for that matter, and it initially suited his fight with Khomeini because as a Muslim group, Khomeini had fewer grounds to attack them ideologically. But Rajavi didn't want the negative points of being Muslim when in the West. Anyway, his role model was Mao. So there emerged the dilemma of whether it was permissible to shake hands, whether hijab should be relaxed or tightened, and whether male members should wear ties in meetings with Westerners.

One explanation given for wearing hijab is that you have to be as holy as Khomeini in order to expose Khomeini's Islam as bad and Rajavi's Islam as good. The organisation can't afford to be involved in any scandal, no matter how slight, or even to look as though it is – that is, from a Muslim's point of view. So strict adherence to Islamic tenets is required, even though this wasn't true at the beginning of the organisation's existence, and later also became untrue because of the Ideological Revolution and marriage, although the deception was carried on for quite a while among the supporters. The logic behind this is that the more corrupted you become as an organisation, the more pure you have to look to the world and in particular, to your followers. This all got confused when the divorces and separation of children started because these ideas are totally counter to Islamic beliefs.

It is worth mentioning Rajavi's other motive for removing and then burning all of the books from the camp libraries and safe houses abroad, (libraries which incidentally only had approved books in them anyway), and that is that these books and documents were in contradiction to having an ideological leader. Even his own speeches in Tehran University in the political phase before 30th Khordad were destroyed. These speeches had been published and avidly read at the time. Their essence was taken from Marx and Mao and was to compare the evolution of species with the evolution of society and, of course, Islamicise it. Another reason was that these books and documents were very much in contradiction with capitalism and harmful to Rajavi's new approach to his new Western masters. Until now, the whole ideology and activities of the Mojahedin, including the killing of Americans, all their songs etc, had been built on Maoism and the fight against the West and imperialism.

These cult-like activities are not new. Rajavi has built his path on the example of Chairman Mao of China and has tried to copy as much as possible of his ideology. As much as ninety percent of it has come from Mao, the remaining ten percent, Rajavi has gleaned eclectically from books on psychology and politics. He very much likes to copy people. In one phase he modelled himself on Yassir Arafat, trying to act, talk and walk like Arafat. Later, after going to Iraq, his role model became Saddam Hussein, except Rajavi isn't built the same as Saddam and the smallest possible gun and holster had to be found for him to wear or it would have looked too big.

Dissent

In direct proportion to the extremes of intrusion, which these mind control techniques use, is the increasing harshness in the treatment of objectors. For the Mojahedin, if you kill someone it does not matter because Rajavi will forgive you. Instead the worst sin a Mojahed could possibly commit is to want to leave the organisation. This is seen as a rejection of Rajavi and that is unforgivable.

At every phase of the Ideological Revolution and during every major event such as Forouq-e Javidan and the Gulf War –

particularly with the removal of children and involvement in suppressing the Iraqi Kurdish population – there have been members who wished to leave the organisation. Dissatisfaction with the political or military policies or the harsh conditions are common reasons. But as time has passed and recruitment dwindled to almost nil, Rajavi has become increasingly reluctant to relinquish his hold on any member. Other and quite pressing reasons exist also. It was dangerous to allow disaffected individuals to be sent to live freely in the West. Many had knowledge of the Mojahedin's intimate relations with the Iraqis, their involvement in many crimes and illegal acts, and above all they had knowledge of Rajavi's use of psychological manipulation techniques. Previously, those who wished to leave had mostly been sent to the refugee camp in Ramardi near Baghdad, but from around 1990 and the Internal Revolution, the growing trend (which was already being practiced) was to imprison dissenting members in special buildings in the Mojahedin's camps.

Rajavi believed that if he only held on to them long enough, he could bully and harass some of these people into once again accepting his leadership. The tools for keeping people obedient are both psychological and physical. This is not difficult to achieve if the person is kept isolated in a camp in Iraq where all contact with the outside world is denied them. The method is very similar to that employed in prisons where gangs operate and prisoners are compelled to join one or another or suffer consequences only slightly more dire than those which force them to choose in the first place. But when obedience to Rajavi breaks down, it gives rise to immense anger. The person gets in touch with their primal survival instinct and this gives a power to resist which is immune to Rajavi's games.

The imprisonment and mistreatment of dissenting members has led to suicide, and murder. Former members, who escaped the Mojahedin in 2002, after years of imprisonment, have reported witnessing two other imprisoned dissenters being beaten to death in one of the Mojahedin's camps. The difficulty for some members, especially those at the highest ranks and who have been members for over two decades, is that they do not wish to leave, they want to continue with the struggle against the Iranian regime. Their objections are based on Rajavi's leadership and their criticism of the mistakes he has made. This might not even constitute a challenge to his right to lead the organisation. (Those who have been close to Rajavi at least recognise the abilities he does have).

Although the criticisms are based on tactical failures, no such thing is allowed inside the Mojahedin. These individuals are subjected to a more specialised form of mental pressure in which feelings of intense guilt are induced in the person's mind. In this state they are shut alone in a room and told there is a cyanide pill available. In most cases, the person has succumbed to this forced suicide as their only way out. One of those alleged to have been a victim of this method is Ali Naghi Had'dadi, known as Commander Kamal. He wanted to continue the struggle under Rajavi's leadership, but he also wanted to have contact with his wife, whom he loved. Although he wasn't a very high ranking member, the success of Rajavi's ideological revolution rested on the acceptance of his decrees by members without exception. He gave Naghi Had'dadi no other choice but to commit 'honourable' suicide.

The latest reports from former members who have escaped the Mojahedin's camps in Iraq, state that dissenting members are now being transferred without any legal process whatsoever, to Iraqi political prisons run by the Iraqi Intelligence and Security Services. There they are subjected to the normal range of abuses associated with such a prison; rape, beatings, and deprivations, which are exacerbated by the fact that they are 'foreigners' and that they have shown disloyalty to the Mojahedin, which the Iraqis consider as part of their own military capacity. In January 2001, some fifty of these prisoners were sent back to Iran under an agreement between Iran and Iraq to exchange POWs. This was certainly a plan of Rajavi's to send them to certain death.

These are surely disturbing reports concerning an organisation which presents itself as the foremost critic of Iran's human rights record, and an organisation which purports to promote women's rights and democracy. It has become clear that most of those who have left did so because they were loyal to their understanding of what the Mojahedin organisation originally represented. The fact is that Rajavi moved the organisation away from its original form and made it into something unrecognisable for these people. It is they who have remained loyal to the Mojahedin, not Rajavi.

The Mojahedin are almost exclusively based in Iraq. When Maryam returned from Europe, Rajavi said that they would stay there until the overthrow of the regime. That includes those who have become disaffected and want to leave. There were many who accompanied Maryam to Paris, but who hadn't the courage or wherewithal to leave at that time and have now found themselves trapped in Iraq with no hope for the organisation or themselves. Quite commonly people are afraid of leaving, even those who have the opportunity. The members of the Mojahedin are people whose mental capacity has been deliberately reduced and for whom there has been induced a debilitating emotional dependence on the leaders. Without this fear, many more of Maryam's entourage would have left while in Europe.

As I have tried to show in this book, Rajavi perverted the ideology of the Mojahedin from its original conception to something, which allowed him total control of all aspects of the organisation including the personal lives of the members. Alongside this internal change, the organisation also lost its direction in the political scene. These two features go hand in hand and the leading element was Rajavi's quest for power. His basic miscalculation was to imagine that if he could impose total power on his members, he would be able to spread this into the rest of Iran and eventually the world.

Chapter 15

POLITICAL SCENE

In 1995 Maryam Rajavi finally gave up on her attempt to re-emerge in the political scene of Europe. She packed her bags to fly back to Iraq. Months previously, it had become clear that she would have to go. So in a last ditch attempt to rescue her mission and in order to save what little face was left for her and the Mojahedin, she spent huge amounts of money on a visit to Norway and the Earls Court concert. But this had little effect and she was forced to return to Rajavi empty handed. Rajavi was furious and severely humiliated and criticised her. Of course, that is something he always does to his followers when they make mistakes, which might cost him his reputation. To stem the flow of members who had begun to leave in disillusion, Rajavi recalled nearly all the Mojahedin members to Iraq, leaving only the close supporters in the European offices to continue with the diplomacy and PR work and the personnel work. Rather than cashing in on the gains made during Maryam's visit, it was all they could do to keep as many supporters or sympathisers as possible loyal.

During July 1995, shortly after the Earls Court concert, Maryam in a pre-arranged private gathering made a speech to British parliamentarians about acts of terrorism committed by the Iranian regime. The issue of women was now replaced by the terrorist nature of the regime. A few months after that in February 1996 Zahra Rajabi, a leading woman member of the

Cf Special Rep re Turkish court verdict 24 Jan 1997 re Reza Barzegar Massoumi A/52/472 15 Oct 1997

Mojahedin, was assassinated in Turkey along with a male Mojahedin supporter, in an apartment they both occupied. The regime denied any involvement in this action. Many began to question; was this organised by Rajavi in a hideous attempt to get Maryam's failed mission back on track? So tainted had the Mojahedin's reputation become among Iranians that they could easily believe that this was part of a plan to put aside Maryam's issue of women and the Mojahedin back on the political track, talking about the crimes of the regime. Of course among the Mojahedin's close supporters other speculation was rife, and all kinds of rumours began circulating. The most popular was that Zahra was involved with the man and was pregnant, something totally unacceptable to Rajavi and his vision for women. People thought they had to be killed because they would not co-operate with what was required of them.

The Mojahedin were facing their worst ever political disaster. Rajavi had fielded the NCRI with Maryam as President elect, to create a new 'brand' image for the Mojahedin, which was rapidly being sidelined by the West in their approaches to Iran. The experiment had been a dismal failure. Maryam failed to gain any political support, whether Iranian or Western. She had almost destroyed the image of the Iranian Resistance by pushing her ideological message at the expense of a political one. Worse than this, her trip had resulted in the loss of around a third of the members she had taken with her from Iraq. Disillusioned with her approach, those brave enough to face the truth, had seen through the hollow facade of the NCRI and left.

The long-suffering supporters living in the West could only stand aside and wait for the dust to settle to see what directive they were to follow next. Rajavi began to recall as many members as he could back to Iraq, and tried to trap the few non-Mojahedin NCRI members there too. In a desperate attempt to cut his losses, and stop the haemorrhaging of disaffected members, Rajavi declared that they would stay in Iraq until the overthrow of the regime.

As a diversion from this political failure, Rajavi announced a new wave of armed resistance activity. But this was to have even worse consequences. Around 1998/9 the Mojahedin began to send operational units of three to five people into Iran, to carry out various military attacks. But this went horribly wrong. The organisation was so heavily infiltrated by now, that four out of every five units were arrested once they were barely over the border. Any unit, which did manage to penetrate into Iran and perform an attack, was arrested soon after. What was most surprising about this situation was that their captors did not kill the invaders. This was a new development in the regime's response to the Mojahedin. Those units who had not performed any military action were, after interrogation, eventually returned to their families inside Iran after giving guarantees that they would not continue their military activities. Those who did manage to perform any military action were arrested, imprisoned and charged accordingly. They were put on trial for the crime they had committed and required to serve any resulting prison sentence.

This version of events was completely new, and was clearly a result of President Khatami's new approach to the threat of the Mojahedin. He had decided to deal with these people not as had previously been the case, as deadly enemies of the country who should de facto be sentenced to death. Rather he treated them as the victims of Rajavi's ambitions, except where they had actually performed a crime in which case the courts dealt with the crime. Khatami was true to his word. The rule of law must prevail.

But this is not what Rajavi had planned or expected. He believed and so did the people who volunteered for the operations, that they would not survive. They went on these missions believing that either they would be killed in the action, or killed by enemy fire or that they would be required to kill themselves with cyanide, should they be in danger of capture. Yet none of the dreadful things which they imagined would happen, did happen.

At one point, the Mojahedin were so certain that one of the women sent on a mission into Iran had been killed, that they printed her obituary in their newspaper. It was only several months later that they discovered she had been captured alive and was serving a prison sentence for her activities. The

Mojahedin quickly recalled all the copies of the newspaper and reprinted a new version with exactly the same date and content apart from the obituary. They deleted the woman from the organisational memory.

The other problem Rajavi faced was that he remained totally under the control of Saddam Hussein. In 1999, Iraq and Iran began a series of communications, which was to lead to a tentative truce between them. As a result, Iraq allowed carefully selected Iranians to visit Iraq's holy Shiite shrines for pilgrimage. Iran in turn gave some covert help to sell Iraqi oil outside the United Nations sanctions. Also in the agreement was the exchange of some POWs from both sides. This rapprochement put an end to Rajavi's plans to increase his military activities, after all, Saddam Hussein controlled the borders not he.

After 11th September 2001, Rajavi refused to make any public statement concerning the tragedy in New York. Quoting from a Persian proverb, he told his followers in a meeting, 'do not ask me to comment upon or analyse the event, the wall has a hole and in that hole is a mouse and the mouse has two ears.' He knew that anything he said in relation to the event would be made public, and so he said nothing. But for those who were in the meeting, his expression made clear his delight. In public, in the Mojahedin's newspapers and other media, there was silence. But Rajavi was too shrewd to miss the import of this terrorist act and the US and international response to it. When the lines were drawn – either you are with us or against us – and when the US liberated Afghanistan, Rajavi must have understood that he personally had no future in Iraq, and that the Mojahedin would be crushed or torn apart in the future if they stayed.

Rajavi is nothing if not pragmatic. Just the opposite of the ideological image he uses to control his members. He sees no contradiction in his followers singing the old Mojahedin song 'war with America' after 9/11, and at the same time sending his envoys to court political support in the USA and Europe. This of course, is in an attempt to broker a deal for his eventual resettlement in one of these countries. He wants to save his own life and he does this by saving the life of the organisation. The two are indivisible.

Since 11th September 2001, Rajavi has made deliberate moves toward rapprochement with the West. He needs to have Western support even though ideologically Rajavi rejects the West's position. Yet Rajavi is faced with what might appear an insurmountable difficulty in his quest for Western support.

Western relations with the Mojahedin have been deteriorating since 1991 when Rajavi chose to remain in Iraq during the allied bombing of Iraq. In spite of the clear defiance of the West's position implicit in this decision, and not forgetting that the Mojahedin acted as apologists for Saddam Hussein during the Iran–Iraq war by denying that he had used chemical weapons against Iranian forces at the battle front, Rajavi tried to brazen his way out of the situation. Even when Human Rights Watch revealed that Mojahedin forces had been deployed to crush a Kurdish rebellion in the north of Iraq, Rajavi was unrepentant.

In October 1991 a military parade was held in Ashraf camp, sixty kilometres north of Baghdad. This parade purported to be a show of strength by the Mojahedin. It was Rajavi's way of keeping himself in the game. He needed the West to continue needing a military threat to the Iranian regime. In an unusual step, journalists were invited and were granted access to question Rajavi as he walked from his car to the platform where he would oversee the parade. For the first time in several years, journalists were able to ask 'when will the regime be overthrown', Rajavi's reply 'sooner than you think' was as cryptic as it was evasive. (Previously, when Rajavi left Iran he told a journalist in Paris they would return in two years. Maryam too, when she left London and returned to Baghdad said the overthrow of the regime would occur within two years.)

In April 1992, the Iranian regime sent fighter jets over the Mojahedin's bases in Iraq and launched several bombs into them. Rajavi's response was instantaneous. Within hours, Mojahedin personnel launched simultaneous arson attacks on Iranian embassies in thirteen Western countries. It was the same tactic as had been used in the early 1980s when the Mojahedin occupied the Iranian embassies in several capitals. In both instances, Mojahedin personnel were sent to prison for up to three months and then deported to the country which had originally granted them refugee status. In both instances, these personnel were immediately back in action, undaunted and using false documentation to continue their activities.

As reports of these activities reached the Intelligence Services of Western countries, concerns began to grow about the true nature of the Mojahedin's relations with the Iraqi regime. Also about whether the organisation could be trusted to remain within the sphere of influence of those who wanted to protect Western interests in the Middle East. Recent activities of the Mojahedin pointed to the emergence of a very different pattern.

In 1994 the United States Foreign Affairs Committee commissioned the State Department to make a report on the Mojahedin. The results were damning. Far from defining the organisation as the benign friend of America and democracy, it was described in the report as terrorist in nature and operating as a personality cult based around Massoud Rajavi's leadership. The Mojahedin were typically scathing in response. Without addressing the concerns highlighted by the report the Mojahedin vilified it as 'whitewashing the mullahs' crimes'.

By 1997 the US government had made its decision on the Mojahedin. They were not to be trusted. In October, Secretary of State Madeleine K. Albright, designated the Mojahedin as a terrorist organisation according to the Anti-Terrorism and Effective Death Penalty Act of 1997. The Mojahedin immediately began a legal appeal against the designation. Again, they accused the Americans of appeasing the Iranian government, but this completely ignored the consistent American position, which was working to maintain sanctions against Iran. Despite the Mojahedin accusations, it is clear that the USA has made no real efforts to mend relations with Iran.

The Mojahedin argued that the so-called terrorist attacks on Iran were legitimate because they only targeted military bodies, and that their actions were confined to Iran as part of a legitimate resistance against the regime's repression. The

Americans, however, had clear evidence that civilians had been killed and injured in the attacks. As though believing their own propaganda, the Mojahedin ignored world opinion and launched 'Operation Great Bahman' in February 2000 with a dozen military attacks against Iran. In 2000 and 2001, the Mojahedin was involved regularly in mortar attacks and hit-and-run raids on Iranian military and law enforcement units and government buildings near the Iran–Iraq border.

By 2000, the United Kingdom had also listed the Mojahedin as a proscribed organisation under the Terrorism Act 2000. In May 2002, the European Union also placed the Mojahedin on its list of terrorist entities. The situation for Rajavi looked bleak.

Undaunted, the Mojahedin continued to operate in the West as the National Council of Resistance of Iran. This is where Rajavi's idea to expand the NCRI with ideologically loyal Mojahedin members began to pay dividends. If Maryam's trip to Europe had been a failure, no matter. He could continue without her to court political support. Rajavi was desperate for a way out of the impasse he found himself in. On one side, his armed resistance activities were failing because of infiltration and because Saddam Hussein controls his military activities from Iraq. On the other side, the Mojahedin was labelled as terrorist. As Western pressure began to build against Saddam Hussein and the accusations of support for renegade terrorist organisations began to fill newspaper columns Rajavi realised that if he stayed in Iraq, he and the Mojahedin would be finished. In November 2001, in a gathering of around 500 top Mojahedin members, he announced his plan, appropriately called the 'Black Phase'.

According to Rajavi, if the United States of America, with or without allies, attacked Iraq, the Mojahedin would have no choice but to launch their biggest ever operation and attack Iran. This would be the best opportunity since Forouq-e Javidan in 1988, for such an attack. Of course he said that, as usual, they would need the permission of the Iraqi government. After years of promises and no sign of progress, this is also Rajavi's best plan to silence any criticism which might be beginning to emerge in spite of the internal repression imposed on all of the members. He will be able to blame external events, that is a war in Iraq, for the necessity of such an action. The vital difference, however, between this and Rajavi's previous attempts to grasp power in Iran, is that this time he knows it will be a futile and suicidal mission. Because of this, Rajavi has also announced that he and his wife Maryam, along with around 300 carefully chosen members, will leave Iraq and make a new base in the West. From there they will be able to reorganise the Mojahedin and maintain their activities beyond the hindrances of the war. Surely no one, but the brainwashed members of the Mojahedin could interpret this in any other way than as a desperate bid on Rajavi's part to escape and save himself, leaving the body of the organisation to be killed or captured by the Iranians.

In 2002, Rajavi started to put his plan into action. He plied the UN Office of the High Commissioner for Refugees in Iraq, to allow selected Mojahedin members to be transferred to Europe and the USA as refugees. Once there, they began their activities. The most important for Rajavi was that they lobby political opinion back in their favour. In spite of this not being a NCRI issue, these loyal followers obeyed Rajavi's directives and began to lobby parliaments and Congress as NCRI members.

They have not been alone in performing this task. The Mojahedin have power and as such they have people who are willing to do their bidding. These include Senators Robert G. Torricelli, Dan Burton, Gary L. Ackerman, James Traficant in the USA, Lord Robin Corbett of Castle Vale, Lord David Alton, Lord Tony Clarke, Lord Archer of Sandwell and Steve McCabe in the UK, as well as Joachim Tapfe and Arne Forman in Germany and Eve Bonet ex-MP in the Assemble Nationale in France. Likewise politicians and parliamentarians in Italy, Luxembourg, Sweden and Norway appear in the list of their active supporters.

In the USA, Senator Torricelli is alleged to have received financial reward from a person associated with the Mojahedin. In the UK, people such as Win Griffiths, MP and Lord Robin Corbett show active support for the Mojahedin's position. What is behind this discord? Are these members really acting in ignorance of the Mojahedin's activities? Have the government departments been unable to brief members sufficiently to warn them off such support?

Let us step back a little from politics and look at what actually comprises the Mojahedin's power. It can be stated with certainty that they have virtually no support from Iranians, either inside Iran or in the West among exiles and émigrés. As regards membership, Rajavi has at his disposal, a totally loyal and self-sacrificing force of up to three thousand people who are willing to perform any task or deed he requires without question. One of the most important of these tasks has been a concerted and prolonged fund-raising campaign. For nearly two decades, the Mojahedin have been collecting money under the disguise of charity work for victims of Iranian repression, earthquakes and floods. Everyone who becomes involved with the Mojahedin is required to take part in fund-raising activities. This means standing in the street in all weathers, all day and asking the public for money. In the evening, a door to door collection is also employed. Collectors are urged to make up any deficit in their daytime amount in these evenings by working even harder. So important has this fund-raising become that classes are held to teach newcomers how best to manipulate the 'subject'. Fund-raising very early on became a litmus test for support. Only those prepared to undergo the hardship and difficulty of this activity, were regarded as ready to move on to the next stage of involvement.

In the UK in 1996, the Charity Commission began an extensive investigation into the charity, Iran Aid. The charity was put into the hands of a receiver and was eventually closed in 1997.

In Germany, the government uncovered the Mojahedin's financial activities. After a two year investigation, the German High Court on 21st December 2001 closed the Mojahedin 'shop' – twenty-five houses and bases – after evidence was found of misuse of Social Security and fraud. Disturbingly, the Mojahedin had used the members' children who had been evacuated during the Gulf War of 1991. These children, whilst they lived in the Mojahedin's bases in Germany, were required to undertake work in the base and take part in fund-raising activities, collecting money in the street. At the same time, the Mojahedin were abusing every possible avenue of Social Security in Germany in order to claim benefits for these children. Documents in Germany showed that ten to twelve million Marks had been used by the Mojahedin to buy weapons. Considering that a Social Security claim of 130–260 Marks could be made per child per day, this is a conservative figure of the amount that the Mojahedin collected on account of these children.

The Mojahedin have also brought to Europe some of their more elderly members who can no longer cope with the harsh conditions in Iraq. These people are also used in fund-raising. That is, standing in the streets from morning until night collecting money under the guise of Iran Aid. These elderly people have little other choice considering the pressures on them.

When Maryam came to Europe in 1993, she brought with her a totally dedicated force who undertook any task required. They set about taking over from the supporters' role of fundraising. With their bullying tactics, their productivity far exceeded anything seen before. Some were able to return up to £1,500 per day. But even before this, in one year alone, Iran Aid charity in the UK had a declared income of £5 million. Its undeclared income has been estimated at over twice this, making a total of over £15 million in one year. If this amount is multiplied for just ten countries: UK, USA, Canada, France, Germany, Italy, the Netherlands, Sweden, Norway and Denmark, then an annual amount of £150 million can be estimated to have made its way to the Mojahedin organisation. If this is multiplied over ten years, then the figure of £1.5 billion gives a rough estimate of the resources which Massoud Rajavi has amassed through the efforts of his devoted followers only in the streets of the West.

Of course, as with any cult, the members are not the beneficiaries of this wealth. It is believed to be under the direct disposal of Rajavi, which would make him one of the world's richest men. In addition, countries such as Saudi Arabia, have generously funded the Mojahedin's struggle. Since the beginning of their exile in the West, Rajavi has constantly urged the supporters inside Iran to send help in the form of gold, jewellery, carpets and money. The Mojahedin's expenses are few. For years France paid their expenses at their base in Paris. Saddam Hussein of course has provided generously, giving them military camps, training, equipment and armoury, food, clothing, etc. General Vafigh Samerai, former Director of Iraqi Military Intelligence, revealed that just one payment to Rajavi amounted to $8 million, and that in addition he received foreign currency to pay for his propaganda activities in the West. In Europe, the Mojahedin's safe houses are funded by Social Security benefits claimed by the members who claim asylum in various countries under various guises.

It is this financial strength then which most reasonably explains the Mojahedin's continued power. Rajavi can pay his way out of trouble, pay for expensive lawyers, and most importantly, can influence at least some of those in power to work his bidding.

We have already seen that Rajavi is unable to compromise or work in collusion with anyone, but that he is willing to act as a mercenary to achieve his own goals. Now we can see that he has power, both financial and forces. This is what makes him a danger. Not though to Iran or the people of Iraq. Rajavi is a danger to Western societies. As he becomes more desperate to regain his foothold on the political scene, there is no way of knowing to what lengths he might go to make his mark. During the Gabon crisis, the Mojahedin threatened the French government with episodes of people setting fire to themselves. In Iran itself, they have conducted a wave of suicide bombings to kill their opponents. Do we know now that the stakes have risen or not?

GLOSSARY

Mojahedin-e Khalq

Refer to themselves in English as the People's Mojahedin Organisation of Iran. Also known as the MKO, MEK, PMOI and NLA. Mojahedin is found alternately spelled as Mujahedin, Mujahidin, Mujahideen, etc.

Ideological Revolution

The name Rajavi gave to his internal coup on the Mojahedin in 1985 when he declared himself and his new wife Maryam as co-leaders, putting aside the Central Committee.

Anti-liberalism revolution

Name given to the Mojahedin activities outside Iran after Rajavi came to Paris as the Mojahedin strove to maintain their revolutionary identity. Any person or organisation which did not take their position as regards Khomeini – ie either him or us – was labelled 'liberal' and condemned by the Mojahedin as betraying the people's legitimate resistance. In spite of claiming to support democracy, the Mojahedin still pursue this approach with other Iranian opposition groups and personalities.

Internal revolution

Second phase of Massoud Rajavi's Ideological Revolution. He demanded that all the members give up their sexuality and devote themselves exclusively to him. He ordered married couples to divorce. Rajavi gave up leadership of the Mojahedin and declared himself Ideological Leader of the whole resistance movement.

Neshast

Literal translation is a 'sitting'. Used to describe Rajavi's system of meetings, though which he controls the Mojahedin's activities and the thoughts of the members.

Massul

Literal translation is 'responsible'. The word was used by the Mojahedin in prison for a person who was responsible for a particular task. It was transferred to the command structure in the Mojahedin to refer to a member who performs any task or who supervises other people. Everyone in the Mojahedin has a massul, that is the person to whom at any one time they must answer and who gives them orders. The massuls represent the hierarchy of control over everything and everyone in the Mojahedin which eventually ends at Rajavi himself.

BIBLIOGRAPHY

Amnesty International Report 2002, 2002, Amnesty International Publications, London

Irfani, S., *Revolutionary Islam in Iran,* 1983, Zed, London

Haworth, *I., Cults: A Practical Guide,* 2001, Cult Information Centre (UK), London